DR. GREG NIELSEN

Gateway to Stardust

How to Resonate with Natural Order Frequencies
Mythological Themes in Art, Literature
and Tattoos

Awakening Series & Book Design by C. Bogard

Conscious Books
316 California Avenue, Ste. 210
Reno, Nevada 89509
U.S.A.

ISBN 978-09619917-3-9

Layout Design & Awakening Series by C. Bogard
Creative Consultant, Certified Marketing & Web Design
Website: http://www.cyndeebogard.com

Email: spiritualfrequenciesonline@gmail.com

Website: http://spiritualfrequencies.weebly.com/

Facebook: https://www.facebook.com/Spiritual-Frequencies-Online-Academy-1436072066656123/?ref=bookmarks

Instagram: drgfrequencies

Twitter: @FrequenciesDrG

YouTube Channel: https://www.youtube.com/channel/UCA8Rwm6Xl-4C8D131dqAkeIw

Become a Patron starting at $3/month at Patreon.com/spiritualfrequencies

Venmo: contribute directly to Conscious Books and Spiritual Frequencies Online Academy: @Greg-Nielsen-9

OTHER BOOKS BY DR.GREG NIELSEN:

STAR CONSCIOUSNESS

RIVERSPEAK

METABUSINESS: CREATING A NEW GLOBAL CULTURE

TUNING TO THE SPIRITUAL FREQUENCIES

BEYOND PENDULUM POWER

PENDULUM POWER

PYRAMID POWER

DIGITAL BOOKS AVAILABLE ON PATREON -

patreon.com/spiritualfrequencies

CREATIVE LIVING

RIGHT LIVING

SANE LIVING

FUNCTIONAL MIND TRAINING

METABUSINESS COMMENTARIES

HOW TO HANDLE THE WORK-A-DAY WORLD 1

HOW TO HANDLE THE WORK-A-DAY WORLD 2

ORGANICS: COMMENTARY ON PSYCHOLOGY

BEGINNING ORGANICS

THOUGHTS ON THE LIGHT

Table of Contents

PART ONE

HOW TO RESONATE WITH NATURAL ORDER FREQUENCIES

Chapter One
The Breathing Spiral

Breathing Spiral blood,
Twisting, turning DNA
Flesh, bones and marrow
Intertwining whirling dervish.

Breathing Spiral life force
Undulating mighty kundalini power
Feel the energy in, through and around
Vibrating cosmic field of dreams.

Breathing Spiral light
Pulsing, traveling photons
In galactic eddies of the mind
Shooting starfire burning bright.

Breathing Spiral – inhale/exhale,
God oxygen filling and emptying.
Soul lungs of refined transparent light.
The Presence, All That Is – meditating.

Opus 1: For and entire day notice the geometry of your actions. For example, when you walk or drive somewhere do you go in a perfect straight line? Or, do you walk or drive in relative straight lines? Try to do everything in "exact" straight lines – walk, pickup things, eat, sit, etc. It will take a major concentrated effort. Imagine drawing your arms, legs, head and body movements on a piece of paper. What would they look like?

Twists & Turns – Your Spiral Growth

How much of your day goes exactly according to plan? Notice what happens today. Notice the twists and turns. How do you feel when things don't go the way you hoped? Are you upset, frustrated, annoyed, angry? Do you welcome the unexpected changes? Do you enjoy the serendipity? The twists and turns in your daily life are the spiral pattern of your individual growth.

Yesterday I had a few obvious twists and turns. Before I went out the door I got into a conversation with my roommate. What we were talking about was meaningful to me. I learned something useful.

It was 9:30 before I took off. I planned on running a route that takes about an hour. I wanted to be back about 10:30 so I could get to a meeting by 11:00.

About a mile or two into the run I saw a woman friend of mine out for a walk. I slowed down to say hi. I asked her if I could walk with her. She said okay.

We walked for about an hour. There was no way I was going to get to the meeting on time. Fortunately, the meeting was optional. My friend took a "wrong" turn on our walk so we missed the street she wanted to walk down in order to see a house she liked.

I decided to walk with her until we arrived back to her house. Once we approached her house she asked me if I wanted to come in.

I said okay putting off my run for a few more minutes.

After seeing her house I continued on my run. "Coincidental-ly" I ran past where the 11 o'clock meeting was to take place.

The run went well. I finished the run on a course I like. It was turning out to be a hot summer day. I had to deal with the heat. I originally wanted to run around 9 am because it was cooler. Another friend had called me at about 9. She had finished a letter of recom-mendation for my son to enter the Talent Academy at school.

I told her that after my meeting I'd come by and pick it up. She told me it would be at her office. I said I'd come by about 12:30. During my run she had called and left a message. I called her back. One of her office appointments had been cancelled. She now wanted me to stop by her apartment to pick up the letter of recommendation.

I could go on and on. Several more things did not go accord-ing to plan that day. Notice the twists and turns in your day, in your life.

Every spiraling twist and turn is your life unfolding, growing, evolving. How you meet and greet the unexpected has much to do with the quality of your life.

The Law of the Breathing Spiral

Nothing goes exactly according to plan. That's the plan. The linear, straight-line world is a mental construct. When you observe nature from galaxies to pine trees you see that nothing is perfectly straight. The world we live in is non-linear, a twisting and turning spiral dance of continuous creating.

The universe on all levels unfolds, breaths and grows according to a spiral pattern. Your life unfolds according to the Law of the Breathing Spiral. Through the twists and turns of daily life you gradually become more conscious.

As you become more conscious and you learn from your experiences, you resonate to another vibrational level represented by a new turn on the spiral. You meet similar situations in a totally different way.

Most people are physical/sensory-based humans. Their range of awareness is relatively narrow, mostly only what can be seen, smelled, tasted, touched and heard. Often, even the most intellectually gifted of the physical/sensory based humans will deny the existence of something because there's no hard evidence.

There are relatively few people who are "energy beings." An energy being is acutely aware of subtle vibrations. They feel the energy from people, places, emotions, thoughts, intuitions and inspirations.

They have evolved through the physical/sensory belief system.

Currently, and during the coming decades and centuries, many more will transform from physical/sensory beings into energy beings – from caterpillars into butterflies, from tadpoles into frogs. This book is for them, a kind of guidebook to becoming an energy being.

Even fewer people are "light beings." A light being's awareness is super subtle and multidimensional. Some very select few live in the mainstream societies. Most work silently behind the scenes in retreats, ashrams, monasteries and remote settings.

Their lives are dedicated to the dissemination of knowledge, wisdom, understanding, creativity, unconditional love and compassion. They are not interested in recognition, fame, fortune and the accumulation of things. They are interested in keeping their attention on a higher frequency energy I'm calling "light."

If you ever happen to be fortunate enough to meet a light being, you will know what I mean by the word light. They emanate what the Hindus call darshan, a spiritual presence. You immediately feel at peace. You feel the love and compassion.

If you spend any time around or near them it will accelerate your rate of vibration. In fact, for some, it's a way to initiate the transformational process from a physical/sensory being to an energy being.

As an energy being one is motivated to consciously connect with The Presence. The Presence is the spiral, the twists and turns, the physical/sensory, energy and light all at once. The Presence interpenetrates and permeates everything, every being, every place in the cosmic spiral dance.

A person who consciously connects with the Presence is One – individualized. There are minimal conflicts. There's nothing that has to be achieved in a personal sense. Any unbalanced energies in their auric-field are dissolved, disintegrated and dissipated. Whatever you thought was so important is hardly important at all.

LIGHT WAVE #81

The alchemists have sung,
"The gold is in the dung."
The light is in the dark,
Transmutation builds the ark.

Earth, water, fire, air
Scattered here and there;
Mix, blend and boil
Becomes the anointing oil.

Mercury, Moon, Sun
Planet-forces spun
Into the Robe of Glory,
The start of another story.

A Physical/Sensory Being

Of the billions of people on earth a high percentage, perhaps well over 90%, spend most of their time and expend most of their energy maintaining the physical body. Food, water, clothing and shelter are required in order to stay alive; that's a given.

When there's free time and energy it's usually used to stimulate the senses in a pleasurable way; that's understandable. We all need recreation, enjoyment, relaxation and play as a balance to the efforts required maintaining the physical body.

Physical/sense-based beings often take maintaining the body beyond what is necessary. They eat excessively. Their wardrobe is extensive. Some people don't wear the same outfit twice, ever. Some people have an elaborate home, which requires fulltime help to maintain. Many others are slaves to their home having to work excessive hours in order to make the mortgage payments.

The global economy is driven by greed and consumerism. Sell, sell, sell; buy, buy, buy. People are compelled to accumulate more things they don't need or use. This materialistic behavior arises out of the belief that we are bodies only. We are not aware of how limited our senses are. We see. We assume that's it. We don't consider that the visible light spectrum is extremely narrow and limited.

There's more to life than the needs of the body. To learn, to evolve, to grow – once the basic bodily needs are met, we are here to learn all we can mentally, emotionally and spiritually.

When we learn we change the way we do things, we make adjustments that make life more fulfilling, joyful, playful and spiritually rewarding. You need to value the needs of the inner spiritual self as much if not more than the needs of the body.

Consumer culture does not value the inner need to evolve by loving, understanding, choosing to be conscious and cultivating wisdom. There's lots of media hype, lip service, psycho-fads and religious babble that will sound and look like what's important. Much is said, very little is done. The "idea" of being aware is not good enough.

Choosing to ignore life's deeper needs does not mean those needs go away. The psycho-logical, deeper self continues to learn, evolve and become more conscious through the seven "Ds" whether we like it or are aware of it or not.

1: Dissatisfaction/Disappointment
2: Depression
3: Divorce/Separation/Lost Love
4: Disease
5: Disaster
6: Danger
7: Death

This unchosen, unconscious learning process is much slower and far more painful. It appears we have "bad" luck. Events appear to happen to us. We don't see the connections between our thoughts, beliefs, feelings and attitudes and the "negative" events we attract.

When one of the seven Ds "happens to us" we go through a period of increased awareness that is usually short-lived. During that time of heightened consciousness we get a glimpse and a feel of another dimension of living. In a sense we are like a seed that is given a glimpse of what it will be like once we sprout and push through the earth into the sunlight.

LIGHT WAVE # 62

Being of celestial fire
Transmute my bestial attire;
Burn the mummy form
Till the light body born.

Dissolve my rigid ways
In liquid light bays;
Cool emotion's heat
In heaven's arctic retreat.

Loosen my earthly ties,
Shine the light on lies;
Remove memory's pain
With love's eternal refrain.

An Energy Being

The next step in evolution on this planet is becoming a functional energy being. For thousands of years there have been initiation orders, which guided a few individuals who were ready to transform from a physical being into an energy being. Now there are hundreds of thousands, if not millions, ready to make, and are making, a leap in evolution.

When I was going through the beginning phases of awakening from the unconscious sleep of automatic sensory living, I was in the hustle and bustle of New York City. I got a job at a textile company with its traditional roots in North Carolina; that's where the manufacturing facilities were located. This was an extremely conservative, hundred-year-old company. You had to be on time, keep your mouth shut and stay focused on work. In fact, if you wanted to go to the bathroom you were asked to wait until your break or lunch time.

As I became more aware of energy I became more sensitive to the vibrational energy fields of places, people and events. Riding the subway, working around unconscious people and handling negative energies became a trial by fire. This was a major test, an initiation, an opportunity to apply what I had learned to keep myself centered and conscious.

What a physical/sensory being saw and experienced as a rou-

tine day of going to work I experienced as an ordeal. It took awareness, courage, guidance and continuous self-discipline to maintain a
semblance of peace and poise.

Entering the workplace I could feel heavy energy unconsciousness in the air. By staying aware of this "heaviness" and not identifying with it I was able to detach from it. If I was tired or not paying
attention, I could feel myself being pulled into the "energy heaviness."
Then I would feel drained. I felt psychically polluted. I could feel
stiffness, tensions and energy blockages. The solar plexus, the neck,
the shoulders, the jaw and the back for me were particularly suscepti-
ble to this heaviness (tension) settling in.

Sometimes I could feel a kind of mental fog settling into and
through my head. Along with this fog I'd often experience a tighten-
ing across the forehead. Other times I'd feel a pulsating heat in the
back of my neck accompanied by a tightness and pressure.

A physical being automatically interprets tensions, headaches
and neck pain as physical problems that need to be attended to by a
physician. If the doctor finds nothing wrong he/she might say they're
"stress" related.

An energy being interprets tensions, headaches and neck pain,
etc. first as an energy blockage. The energy had become congested.
From an energy perspective, if you change the rate of vibration from a
slower rate to a faster rate the blockages tend to release and the energy
will flow.

I practiced and learned a vast variety of skills that assisted me
in changing the rate of vibration.

Here's a list of some of these skills.

1: Rhythmic Breathing
2: Focused Relaxation
3: Self-Observation
4: Diligent Awareness
5: Self-Remembering
6: Transmutation of Energy
7: Conscious Sensory Awareness
8: Energy Follows Attention

9: Detachment and Non-Identification
10: Rhythmic Alternation
11: The Law of Three
Etc.

By learning, practicing and mastering these skills you become an Energy Being. You go through a rapid evolutionary shift in consciousness. You connect with the Energy World and learn to navigate in and through it.

A Light Being

After writing Beyond Pendulum Power, I was invited to speak in Fort Collins, Colorado. I gave a Friday night talk introducing the pendulum. On Saturday I gave a workshop on how to use the pendulum.

While I was setting up Saturday morning people began to trickle in. It looked like we were going to have a good size group. I could see the entrance to the room clearly from where I was standing so I got a feel for who was arriving.

About ten minutes before I was to start a yogi walked through the door dressed in the traditional yogi attire. Immediately I could feel the energy in the room change. It felt more peaceful, uplifting, spiritual.

It didn't take but a few seconds to recognize that an evolved being was going to be with us. We exchanged greetings. I felt fortunate someone evolved and conscious was going to participate. I knew it would be an extra special workshop. It was apparent to everyone attending that it was going to be a blessed experience.

At first, I felt awkward giving a workshop on the pendulum when the yogi "light being" could have given us an enlightening presentation. I encouraged him to share any insights he might have or suggestions that could improve our skill level with the pendulum. Any time he spoke we hung on every word. He was gracious and thoughtful, not wanting to divert the class from the topic at hand.

There are a small percentage of evolved beings that have more or less mastered their energies. They resonate with a dimension (frequency band) I'm calling light. They radiate high frequency energy or light, a presence that tends to induce a more centered, calm and spiritually awakened state. Often a person who is becoming an energy being will attract a light being teacher who will assist them in making the transformation from a physical/sensory being to an energy being. There is not that many light beings around so one is fortunate to come across one.

Most light beings are not out and about working 9-5, raising kids, and making a house payment and shopping at the grocery store. Usually they are connected with an ashram, monastery, retreat or other safe haven where they can focus their purpose, meditate and teach.

Usually a light being is connected with an initiation school where they have gone through a rigorous training over ten, twenty, thirty or more years. Some of the schools I'm aware of include yoga, Tibetan Buddhism, Zen Buddhism, Native American, Egyptian-Coptic and Sufi.

In the past there have been many initiation orders that had light beings including Rosicrucian, Masonic, Alchemical, Inca, Mayan, Aztec, Hawaiian Huna, Aborigine, Greek Gnostic, and Celtic to name a few. There still may be light beings on the planet that train in one of the traditions. I'm just not aware of them.

If you have an opportunity to go to a lecture, talk or meeting given by one of these evolved beings then by all means do so. Many of them have written books. When you read their words you feel a change in energy. You're more aware, relaxed, peaceful, energized and meditative.

SWIRLING FORCE

Troubled swirl of force can dismay
The walker of the straight and narrow way
Negative thought – feeling energy field
The master of force will bend and yield.

Swirling force all men-women receive
Store, radiate till they finally achieve
Control of thought-feeling-will
No more to rape, steal or kill.

Positive force awakens, enlightens
Clearness, purifies and whitens
The energy-force-field soul
In order to make the raiment body whole.

Positive, negative, neutral – threefold force
Triangular form on a spiral course
Focused in multiordinal structured points
Vibrating in body, bone and joints.

Force in atom, molecule and cell,
Energy to cross the ignorance hell
Precious life – essence use wisely
Don't waste or spill, be miserly.

The Presence

An evolved being enjoys silence. They enjoy peace and quiet. For them setting aside time to commune with The Presence is a must.

In order to commune and feel The Presence you need to slow down, stop rushing and spend quiet, alone time. There are so many demands and distractions in daily life it seems next to impossible to find a few minutes of peace and quiet. Yet if you make the time, choosing to be alone, you give yourself the gift of silence. This leads to The Presence – the super-subtle force-vibration behind, in and through everything, person, soul, dimension, etc.

As you read this you are holding a book, sitting comfortably. The Presence sustains the "thing" you are sitting on, chair, bed, couch or whatever. Hold your attention on the "thing" with reverence and gratitude and you'll feel The Presence.

The Presence is intimately involved with every breath, every thought, every feeling. The air, thoughts and feelings are invisible to the physical eyes yet you experience them. The Presence cannot be seen, heard, touched, smelled or tasted but it can be felt. You experience that feeling as you place your attention with reverence and gratitude within the air, thoughts, feelings and things.

Summary

1: The twists and turns in your life are the spiral pattern of your individual growth.

2: How you meet and greet the unexpected has much to do with the quality of your life.

3: The world we live in is non-linear, twisting and turning in a spiral dance of continuous creativity.

4: You evolve according to the Law of the Breathing Spiral.

5: As you become more conscious and you learn from your experience, you resonate with another vibration level represented by a new turn of the spiral.

6: Of the billions of people on earth perhaps well over 90% spend most of their time and energy maintaining the physical body.

7: There's more to life than the needs of the body. To learn, to evolve, to grow – these are fundamental to living.

8: Consumer culture does not value the inner need to evolve by loving, understanding, choosing to be conscious and cultivating wisdom.

9: Choosing to ignore the deeper needs of living does not mean those needs go away. You continue to learn, evolve and become more conscious through the seven Ds.1. Dissatisfactions/Disappointments, 2. Depression, 3. Divorce/Separation/Lost Love, 4. Disease, 5. Disaster, 6. Danger, 7. Death.

10: When we experience one of the seven Ds we go through a time of heightened awareness. We get a glimpse and a feel for another dimension of living.

11: The next step in evolution on this planet is becoming an energy being. This book is mostly for these budding energy beings who are taking responsibility for their own evolution.

12: From an energy perspective, if you change the rate of vibration from a slower rate to a faster rate the blockage will be released and the energy will flow.

13: By learning, practicing and mastering new skills you become an energy being. You connect with the energy frequency world and become more conscious.

14: There are a small percentage of evolved beings on earth that have more or less mastered their energies. They resonate with a dimension (a frequency band) I call light.

15: Often a person who is becoming an energy being will attract a light being teacher who will assist them in making the transformation from a physical/sensory being to an energy being.

16: If you have an opportunity to go to a lecture, talk or meeting given by one of these light beings by all means do so. Many of them have written books and created videos (YouTube). When you read and listen to their words you feel a change in energy.

Chapter 2

You Are an Energy Being

You are an energy being
Living in an energy universe.
Notice what you're seeing:
Observe the material curse.

You are an energy soul
Alchemically transform
Make yourself whole
And weather the sensory storm.

You are energy in time
Seven planetary centers
Whirling in perfect rhyme
Until the light being enters.

They you radiate the light.
Awaken, you sleepyhead.
A beacon in the night
Choose: The Quick or the Dead.

Opus 2: With everything you touch and see say to yourself:
"This is a pattern of energy in a dynamic energy world." Keep it up day and night. Continually touch and see every "thing" as a pattern of energy. If you forget for a while that's okay. Just start up again. From the time you wake up until you go to sleep say, as you touch and see, say, "This is a pattern of energy in a dynamic energy world."

The Energy World

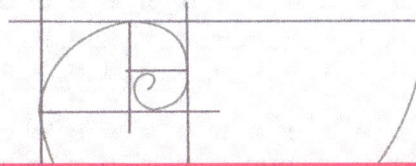

We live in a dynamic energy world. Our senses tell us we live in a physical world of hard, impenetrable things. Our culture tells us that our world is full of material things that we need to buy and sell. And when a material thing wears out, and we don't need it any more, we are told to throw it in the garbage. By first grade we are taught that inanimate objects (things) like rocks, plants and personal possessions are not alive while animate objects like animals and people are alive.

The reality I am writing about is based on current science – quantum physics. We live in a dynamic energy world. Physical, material, hard things are configurations of energy. So-called inanimate objects are, in truth, highly animate.

Itzhak Bentov in his book Stalking the Wild Pendulum writes:

"Well, it seems that real reality – the micro reality, that which underlies all our solid, good, common sense reality – is made up of a vast empty space filled with oscillating energy fields. It's an interlocked web of energy fields, each pulsating at their own rate but in harmony with the others, their pulsations spreading out farther and farther throughout the cosmos."

Is the book you are holding, experiencing, a thing, an inanimate object, a dead piece of matter? As you're holding this book, bring your awareness to your hands. Bring awareness to the contact points between your hands and the book. Say out loud, "This is a pattern of energy in a dynamic energy world." Say it again. Pause. Say it again. Repeat, repeat, repeat until you condition yourself to this world being an energy world.

Notice what you feel, what you register. What are you reactions? Do you feel foolish? Do you think it's a bunch of nonsense? Does a part of you feel like it's obvious that the book is hard matter and not a pattern of dynamic energy?

Your feelings and thoughts are certainly understandable. The culture, the educational system, parents, your sensory experiences have led you to believe that reality is material. Why change? Living life accepting the matter belief seems to work. Or, does it?

When it comes to driving a car it makes sense to accept the world as hard, solid matter. By driving with awareness and obeying the traffic laws you avoid an accident. You better believe your car is hard matter. If it collides with another hard matter car going 60 miles an hour the crash and crunch could kill you.

How about the energy world belief based on scientific evidence? Many people agree mentally, yes, we live in an energy world. They accept the scientific findings. However, accepting an idea doesn't mean one lives and functions in the energy world as a conscious energy being.

Re-educating and re-training your mind-body to the energy world is a process that takes years. It does not happen just because you accept a thought or idea. The process of living as an energy being in a dynamic energy world is accelerated by putting into practice the **OPUS:** With everything you see and touch say to yourself, "This is a pattern of energy in a dynamic energy world."

TEXT POEM 5: FLUID

Easing in and out,
Fluid feelings,
Tides of thought motion.
Energy space stars
And light waves.
Splash across galaxies.
What time do you have?
Tell me without looking
At a clock or smartphone.
Please don't think about it;
Just tell me; say it.
I felt the splash of time
On the beach of space.
Everything is on schedule
And at ease.
Fluid.

The Next Step in Evolution

There are many people on the planet who are budding energy beings. Many of these are not aware that they need to take the "next step in evolution." There are many other people who are aware of energy, to some extent, but do not train in mastering energy.

Just the other day a woman called me with the following story. "My daughter told me I was self-centered and no longer was a good mother. A lot of tension went on between us. I let my daughter know that it was time I got on with my life. After all, she's thirty-five and I'm sixty.

The next day I went away to my home to spend some quiet time. The first day I was there I started hyperventilating to the point that I went to the hospital. I didn't know what was happening. The doctor checked me out and found nothing wrong."

I told her she is picking up on or resonating with an energy. She was experiencing a sympathetic vibration or rapport from her daughter. You could tell she had never heard anything like it before. She did not know what to make if what I said. I told her she as an energy being and needed to learn how to manage her energy.

There are techniques, methods and skills she could use to transform and transmute energy. She had commented to me previously that she had been a sensitive soul all her life. She was a poet and a philosopher.

Some years ago I was walking down a street with a woman friend near where she worked. Suddenly, she said, "I've got a sharp pain in my heart. I think I need to go to the hospital." I told her the pain was a rapport from her mother. She thought I was crazy. She insisted she needed immediate attention from a doctor.

I suggested she take slow, rhythmic, deep breaths through her nose. Again, she thought I was nuts. But the pain was so intense she was willing to try anything. After five or six deep breaths the pain began to subside. She looked relieved. The panic feeling began to leave.

I said, "I'm pretty sure you're picking up a sympathetic vibration from your mother."

She responded by saying, "I don't see how that could be possible."

In the days previous to this incident she had described negative experiences between she and her mother. I asked her to give her mother a call right now to see if my statement was accurate.

She called her mom. You could tell she had the thought, 'I'll prove this guy wrong.' Within seconds of calling her mom she look surprised. After hanging up, she told me her mom was upset with her and had tried calling her a few minutes ago. That was about the time she felt the pain in her heart.

Even though both of these people were sensitive to energy they believed they were physical/sensory beings. When they felt an energy in and through the body, they only knew how to interpret the pain, the energy activity, as a physical problem requiring the immediate care of a doctor. In reality, they are both energy beings requiring training in taking the next step in evolution.

Today there are literally millions of people who do not know they are energy beings. They do not have the information, training, awareness and skills to direct, channel, transform and transmute the different frequencies of energy they pick up on, feel, experience.

There are millions of others who know about and accept the energy world but do not have the knowledge of how to navigate this vast cosmic sea. They have set sail but have little or no knowledge of the currents, the prevailing winds or the plotting of a course using the stars.

The Energy Body

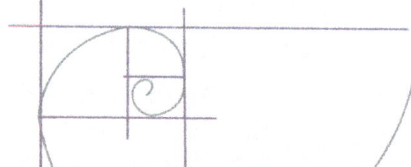

Dr. Andrew Weil writes in his book Spontaneous Healing, "The more you experience yourself as energy, the easier it is not to identify yourself with your physical body." This statement represents a fundamental paradigm shift in our culture. Not only do we "have" a physical body, we "have" an energy body (energy-field).

In, through and surrounding the physical body (physiological organism) is the energy body. Dr. Weil and others in the established medical profession are onto something. Most, if not all, physical diseases begin first in the energy body. If we allow negative emotions, feelings, thoughts and environments to load the energy body with negative experiences, we can expect the physical body to eventually manifest symptoms, ailments and diseases.

Visualize your energy body as your house. If you have any fearful, hateful people living in your house or visiting your house, how do you think that will feel? Will you want to live there?

If you keep all the windows covered and closed you do not allow sunlight and fresh air into your house. Your house will be a dark, dingy place. Will you want to live there?

As an energy being you need to see yourself as an energy-field, as an energy being living in and through your energy being. "The more you experience yourself as energy, the easier it is not to identify yourself with your physical body."

I remember when I began to experience myself more as energy. One day I felt a pressure in my forehead area. I observed myself saying to myself, "I've got a headache." After catching myself identifying myself as a physical body, 'I've got a headache.' I decided to see/feel the experience as energy. I felt a contraction, a lightly painful energy moving into my forehead area.

Choosing to experience the so-called "headache" as energy, I noticed it did not feel as painful, as fixed in my head. In fact, I decided I did not have to identify with it at all. I saw it as energy moving in, through and away. The "headache" was gone as quickly as it came.

Your energy body can actually be photographed. I've had my energy body photographed using Kirlian photography. Each time there has been different colors. One time I had been upset and angry. Red was the dominant color. Another time I had been doing hours and hours of mental work; yellow was my prominent color. Once I purposely meditated for about twenty minutes on violet light before taking the photos; the primary color was violet.

I recently saw an ad in a local paper: Aura Imaging Photography, a camera actually records your electromagnetic energy on film. In 1939, Semyon Davidovich Kirlian, a Russian electrician, designed a camera that photographed living things. When he placed a leaf in a high frequency energy-field, "it revealed a world of myriad dots of energy. Around the edges of the leaf there were turquoise and reddish-yellow patterns of flares."

In 1968, Soviet scientists at the State University of Kazakstan published their findings in a book-long scientific paper, The Biological Essence of the Kirlian Effect. "The bioluminescence visible in the Kirlian photos is caused by the bio-plasma, not the electrical state of the organism." The vibrating, colorful energy body "has a specific organization."

The Kazakh scientists concluded there are patterns of energy in motion inside the energy body that are completely different than the physical body. They also discovered that the air we breathe charges the energy body restoring its equilibrium.

Dr. V. Inyushin, one of the Kazakh scientists, stated at a parapsychology conference in Moscow:

"The Kirlian discovery has opened up the possibility of studying the energy states of the organism. It is through the energy body that we react to all cosmic occurrences. When there are disturbances of the sun (solar flares), biologists have charted all kinds of biological reactions in humans, plants and animals. These disturbances of the sun cause changes in the whole energy balance of the universe and in turn affect the energy of living organisms. This results in the physical changes we can see."

After reviewing the Soviet scientist's research, Sheila Ostrander and Lynn Schroeder wrote in their book, Psychic Discoveries Behind the Iron Curtain:

"It makes you wonder if the Soviets are beginning to uncover in the workings of the energy body some new scientific basis for another ancient system of thought: Astrology."

"If it is actually possible to develop a heightened sensitivity toward celestial influences then it may not be implausible to suggest that the ancients might well have been able to experience (feel) astrological effects directly and routinely by way of the energy body."

The Energy Centers (Chakras)—Planets

"Respecting any given individualized field (energy body), we speak of the seven streams of energy as foci or energy-centers which determine the 'web' or pattern upon which the lines of force configurate or take form." From The Natural Order Process, volume 3, Vitvan.

If you have done any amount of reading, study, research into Eastern philosophies you have come across the term chakras. There are seven chakras or energy centers in the energy-body-field.

In the Western tradition going back to ancient Greece, Egypt, Babylonia, Sumerian, etc., these seven energy centers were the seven planets. The priest astrologers observed a correspondence and resonance with the planets in the solar system and the energy centers in the energy body.

"Many of the ancient seers knew, by direct experience, the relation of the force centers in a given individualized field with the greater concentrations of energy in the solar field." (the planets) Vivtan.

There is also a correspondence between the planets and the days of the week. John B. West writes in The Case for Astrology:

"In all cultures and societies, Sunday is assigned to the Sun, Monday to the Moon, Tuesday to Mars (our English days combine Teutonic and Latin names for the planets/gods concealing the planetary sequence). Tuesday is from the Teutonic 'Tiw' or Mars, Wednesday from Wodin or Mercury, Thursday from 'Thor' or Jupiter. Friday from 'Freya' or Venus and Saturday from Saturn."

Planet /Symbol	Day	Energy Center	Location
Sun ☉	Sunday	Crown	Top of the Head
Moon ☽	Monday	Third Eye	Between Eyebrows
Mars ♂	Tuesday	Solar Plexus	Pit of the Stomach
Mercury ☿	Wednesday	Throat	In the Throat Area
Venus ♀	Friday	Heart	Behind Breast Bone
Jupiter ♃	Thursday	Spleen	Above Sex Organ
Saturn ♄	Saturday	Base Spine	Tail Bone

As you identify yourself more as energy, as you become more conscious of energy, the planets, the energy centers begin to activate, vibrate at a higher frequency. In the beginning phases of becoming an energy being Jupiter, Mars, Venus, Mercury and the Moon accelerate in vibration. You will experience energy as a registration of force in/ through these five centers.

Conscious energy releases sensitive energy. In other words, as you become more aware of your thoughts, feelings, emotions and actions, you become more sensitive. You feel the energy of a person, a place, a "thing" and an event.

Let me tell you from personal experience these centers (planets) are very real. If you choose the path of becoming an energy being or, if the path chooses you, knowing about these centers and how to handle the energy feelings experienced through the centers will save you endless hours of difficulty, pain, confusion, frustration, misunderstandings, etc.

I remember a time when I woke up in the middle of the night with sharp pains in my stomach (physical body term) in the Mars center (solar plexus) energy being term. It felt like a knife was poking into me. At first, I thought I might have the flu or possibly I ate something that didn't agree with me. Notice the thoughts that automatically arise from the culturally ingrained belief that we are physical bodies.

I eventually switched my focus to: I am picking up on some

energy on the Mars level. This simple perceptual change from a physical perspective to an energy perspective lessened the intensity of the
pressure felt in the solar plexus.

As an energy being you will need to learn alchemical, transmuting skills, transforming negative energy into a positive energy. I
began slow rhythmic breathing through the nose to the count of three
in and three out. I noticed the energy moving into and through the
solar plexus area. Remember what the Soviet scientists discovered?
The air we breathe charges the energy body restoring its equilibrium.
At the very instant it impinged/registered through the Mars center I
visualized it as light and saw this energy moving upward as if through
a chimney of light in the center of my energy body.

Higher frequency energy transforms and transmutes lower
frequency energy. In a matter of minutes I felt the "pain" disappear. I
went back to sleep and slept soundly for several more hours.

It's not always that quick and easy. Often, I need to do several other things in order to transform and transmute the energy to
a higher frequency. As you continue reading, I will share as many
techniques, methods, skills, etc. as I can to assist you in becoming a
functional energy being.

I want to mention here that many people who have little or no
experience of feeling energy may react to the energy centers – planets
– in a negative, skeptical, fearful, even angry way. I suggest you avoid
trying to convince, prove or argue the point. In most cases it will be a
futile effort.

The proof is in the pudding. Your personal experience is all
the proof you need. In my opinion it's better to accept and respect
another's viewpoint or belief. Go into mental-emotional neutral and
wish them well in your heart. You will transform and transmute the
negative energy.

You might think of it this way – at one time the majority of
people believed the world was flat. It didn't change the fact that the
world is roundish. If someone believes that energy centers/planets are
some "new age" mumbo-jumbo, it doesn't change the fact that they
are dynamically alive energy focal points within the energy body.

COMMENTS

The signs unknown, unrealized yet
While journeys ended and more ahead
And milestones reached and others passed by
Some seen, some sensed not to forget
While others lost forever
A sudden changing wind has whispered to me and said
"Lost in a place out beyond the visible sky
To chance upon again? Never - never."

Must tranquility and security measure the success
Of life ended and life to come?
Will only material possessions represent achievements?
What purpose do the intangible things possess?
Like imagination, love and happiness
They could help the lacking sensitivity of some.
Upon yourself pass judgments
And live not in emptiness.

What Are You Resonating With?

What is resonance? Itzhak Bentov writes in his book Stalking the Wild Pendulum: "Suppose we tune two violins, then put one of them on the table and play a note on the other. If we watch carefully, we shall see that the same string that we're playing on one violin is also humming on the violin that we placed on the table. Clearly, there is a 'sympathetic resonance' between the two. Let us analyze what is happening. When we draw the bow over a string, it vibrates at its own natural frequency, which we call self-frequency. Since the two violins are correctly tuned, we know that the natural frequencies of both strings were identical. Within a system like this (we shall call the violins a 'system'), it is very easy to transfer energy.
In this case, we are talking about acoustical energy. The airwaves generated by the first violin impinge on the second violin. The string that is tuned to the emitted note will absorb the energy of the waves of that frequency preferentially because that energy comes to it at its own natural frequency. The energy transfer with the system is therefore optimum, and such a system, made up of two tuned oscillators, is called a resonate system."

If the energy you start resonating with has you feeling tired, drained, feeling pains in the intestinal area, solar plexus, heart or head, you may be in rapport, in resonance with an energy that is negative relative to your natural frequency. You become what is called rhythm entrained. Your energy centers are vibrating in unison with say some of the people attending a football game as well as some of the people watching the game on television and listening on the radio. Here's what Bentov writes about rhythm entrainment: "Suppose we go out on a balmy summer evening and notice some fireflies settling in the bush, blinking off and on. At first, this blinking is random, but fairly soon we notice that an order is slowly developing. After a while, we see that the fireflies in the whole bush are blinking on and off in unison. This phenomenon is called rhythmic entrainment. It seems that nature finds it more economical in terms of energy to have periodic events that are close enough in frequency to occur in phase or in step with each other. This is the meaning of rhythmic entrainment."

Becoming conscious what you're resonating with requires a vigilant awareness of the vibrational qualities of your country, culture, community, neighborhood, friends, family, co-workers, and interests like hobbies, sporting activities, reading material, spiritual beings and music. An energy being navigates the energy world by consciously choosing that which enhances, improves, uplifts, rejuvenates and energizes. When an energy being inadvertently, unconsciously and unintentionally chooses to identify with a negative energy/quality, they know what do to detach from that negative frequency.
Vitvan in his Basic Teaching of the Natural Order, volume 3 writes: "When the solar center (Mars energy center) is opened, susceptibility to environmental frequencies is greatly enhanced; and since the racial forces are concentrated on this level, the frequencies registered, pertaining to the present racial stages and states, may be most disturbing and destructive. So when one finds that this center is opening and he is developing a susceptibility to frequency registration which he had never experienced before, of necessity, he has to be more circumspect concerning places, persons, radio (film, television, internet) programs, etc. to which he lends himself."

TEXT POEM 7: ON THE EVE OF YOUR LAST DAY ON EARTH

Time is a smooth current
Washing up and over life.
Leaving behind traces of innocence.
Hiding the truth or
Revealing the pain.
Always flowing, seeking,
Altering its path.
Until the day the moon is high
And its reflection, motionless
On the eve of your last day on earth.
As the last breathe passes your lips.
You're now one with the water
That once lapped your feet.
The time has passed to care.
Or worry or fret.
You are free to ride high
And sing in the space
Full of peace.

Raising Your Vibration

When you're resonating, vibrating with a negative energy, relative to you, one or several of the following may be happening or recently happened.

Drained
Tired for No Apparent Reason
Extremely Tense
Emotionally Upset
Thinking Obsessively
Depressed
Doing Too Much
Around a Public Place for an Extended Time
Around a Negative Person for an Extended Time
Etc.

Resonating with a negative energy lowers your vibration. As an energy being you need to restore harmony; you need to raise your vibration. There are literally thousands of ways to raise your vibration and restore peace, balance and vitality. Remember, the sooner you notice your energy zapped, negative, being drained, etc. and do something effective to transmute the lead into gold, the sooner you'll feel recharged.

1: Be Aware. When you make a habit of noticing what's going on both in your immediate environment and within yourself, you give yourself the opportunity to change what's happening. Unconsciousness, lack of awareness, tends to accept the situation as it is.

2: Detach. In order to detach, not identify with a negative person, place or circumstance, you need to let go. Letting go and detaching requires that you focus your attention on more positive people, places and/or circumstances.

3: Breathe Rhythmically. Breathe slowly through the nostrils. Notice your breathing; just notice. Allow your breathing to be deeper and more rhythmic.

4: Relax. Bring your attention to your neck, your shoulders, your back. Do you notice tense muscles? When you feel a tense area gently bring your attention there. Allow your attention to go slowly into the tension.

5: Meditate. Stop what you're doing even for a few minutes and meditate. Sit in a relaxed, upright position. Notice, without opinion or judgment, the coming and going of thoughts, images, concepts, desires, etc.

6: Connect with Conscious People. Connect, call, spend time with and around people who give you positive energy, encouragement and love. These people are givers, not takers. They listen without criticism and with understanding.

7: Listen to Uplifting Music. If the music slows you down, mellows you out and relaxes you, then it is music that raises your vibration. Contemporary jazz, classical and "new age" are musical categories to consider.

8: Read Uplifting Authors. Notice how you feel when you read certain authors. I know that when I read works written by the Dalai Lama I feel better; it raises my vibration.

9: Listen to Uplifting Authors. Notice how you feel when you listen to certain authors. Audio books and lectures are easily available online, in bookstores and libraries.

10: Commune with Nature. Walk by water, through the woods, in the mountains. If you live in the city, go to a park. Enjoy communing with the trees, the earth and the sky. Feel the warm sun, the wind, the earth under your feet. If possible, go into the ocean, a mountain lake, a meandering stream or river.

Summary

1: We live in a dynamic energy world. Physical, material, hard things are configurations of dynamic energy.

2: Bring your awareness to the contact points between your hands and the book. Say to yourself, "this book is a pattern of energy in a dynamic energy world."

3: Re-educating and re-training your mind-body to the energy world is a process that takes years.

4: There are many people on the planet who are budding energy beings. They are not aware that they need to take The Next Step in Evolution.

5: There are techniques, methods and skills you can use to transform and transmute energy.

6: "The more you experience yourself as energy, the easier it is not to identify yourself with your physical body." Dr. Andrew Weil

7: If you allow negative emotions, feelings, thoughts and environments to load your energy body with negative experiences, you can expect the physical body to eventually manifest symptoms, ailments and diseases.

8: Choosing to experience a so-called headache as energy I noticed it did not feel as painful, as fixed in my physical head.

9: There are patterns of energy in motion inside the energy body that are completely different than the physical body.

10: The air we breathe charges the energy body restoring its equilibrium.

11: "In the workings of the energy body there may be some scientific bases for another ancient system of thought: astrology." Ostrander & Schroeder.

12: "It may not be implausible to suggest that the ancients might well have been able to experience (feel) astrological effects directly and routinely by way of the energy body." John West

13: In the ancient traditions going back to Egypt, Greece, Babylonia and Sumeria, the seven energy centers (chakras) correspond with the seven planets: Sun, Moon, Mercury, Mars, Venus, Jupiter and Saturn.

14: As you identify yourself more as energy, as you become more conscious of energy, the planets, the energy centers begin to activate, vibrate at a higher frequency.

15: Knowing about the energy centers and how to handle the energy experienced through the centers will save you endless hours of difficulty, pain, confusion, frustration and misunderstanding.

16: Higher frequency energy transforms and transmutes lower frequency energy.

17: Your energy centers can absorb the vibrations radiating from the people you come into contact with and the places you go.

18: Becoming a functioning energy being requires that you constantly ask yourself, "What am I resonating with?"

19: If the energy you're resonating with has you feeling tired, drained, feeling pains in the intestinal area, solar plexus, heart or head you may be in rapport with an energy that is negative relative to your natural frequency. You've become rhythmically entrained; you're in rapport.

20: An energy being navigates the energy world by consciously choosing that which enhances, improves, uplifts, rejuvenates and energizes.

21: My top ten ways of raising your vibration include: Be Aware, Detach, Breathe Rhythmically, Relax, Meditate, Connect with Positive People, Listen to Uplifting Music, Read Uplifting Authors, Listen to Uplifting Authors, Commune with Nature.

WANDERING THROUGH THE STARS

Wandering through the stars
Brain cells on fire,
Eyes full of sparks
Matter into light
Taking off the mask
Stage fright
Gasping space
Hydrogen-helium high.
Atomic energy mind
Exploding thought forms.
Creation is continuous
Breathing in and out
Till mind becomes a sun
Warming space and earth.
Hearts flicker with feeling
Radiant life forms changing
Into kingdoms
Mineral, vegetable, animal
Come out of the rock
Go beyond the flower.
Transmute instinct
Conscious of consciousness
Galactic brain waves
High tide – low tide.
Silent waves pounding
Through protons-electrons.
Dissolving subatomic particles
Splashing on solar system beaches
Cosmic tan invisible
Ultra violet feeling
Wandering through the stars.

Chapter 3
Conscious Energy

Focus on conscious energy first;
Experience its natural empowerment.
The unconscious bubble will burst
Loosening the habit world attachment.

Practice self-remembering day and night;
Conscious wordless awareness
Fans the flame of fire light,
Awakens you more or less.

Get to know You.
Observe your thought-talk,
Your action-reaction cue.
Now walk the walk.

Choose the conscious way.
Awaken from hypnotic sleep.
Choose every second of every day
To make the evolutionary leap.

Opus 3: Start your day by saying to yourself:
"I am completely aware in the here-now." Continue with this affirmation morning, noon and night. Choose to be more aware by self-remembering. Continually say to yourself, "I am completely aware in the here-now." Choose to make heightened awareness, being conscious, your first priority in thought, word, action and sensory awareness day in and day out.

Conscious Energy

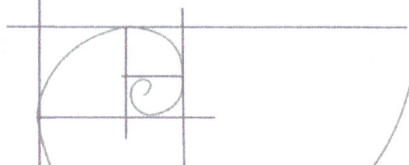

It was a blustery fall Sunday. The late October Minnesota air pierced like a laser through bone. I was home from the University of Minnesota for the weekend. During the quiet morning hours I was studying for exams.

I decided to take a break. I walked back to my bedroom that I shared with my brother Mike. The door was locked. Usually it was open. I knocked. There was no answer. It seemed odd. I looked for a nail small enough in diameter to push through the hole and unlock the door.

I returned with a nail and unlocked the door. Walking in I was stunned, shocked to see Mike lying on the bed lifeless. There was a 22-caliber rifle on the floor and a small bullet wound through the heart. Mike was dead.

Death, one of the seven "Ds." Remember Chapter 1? "When one of the seven Ds "happens to us" we go through a period of increased awareness. The shock of my brother's unexpected and unexplained death catapulted me into a heightened state of acute awareness that lasted for months.

I was keenly aware of every little sound, smell, thought, feeling, word and movement. This state of awareness was dramatically different than the day-to-day automatic sensory awareness that we usually experience. It was as if I'd awakened from a long sleep. Everyday automatic awareness seemed like a deep sleep compared to the heightened, acute consciousness I experienced after my brother's death.

Reflect on your life. Write down events and experiences that you would categorize as one of the seven Ds.

1: Disappointment/Dissatisfaction. Recall a major disappointment. Write it down. How did you feel? Use keywords to describe your awareness, sensitivities and hypersensitivities.

2: Depression. Have you ever been depressed? What were you depressed about? Write down keywords that best describes your depression. What was the quality of your awareness while depressed?

3: Divorced/Lost Love. Have you ever gone through a love breakup from someone you loved deeply? Perhaps you've gone through a divorce. Maybe you've lost a special pet. How would you describe that experience? Jot down some keywords.

4: Disease. Remember the last time you were sick. Have you ever gone through a major illness? Write down keywords that best describe your range of thoughts and emotions. How would you describe the quality of your awareness?

5: Disaster. Natural disasters can dramatically change your awareness. Whether a hurricane, flood, tornado, earthquake, blizzard or forest fire, write down a few keywords describing your experience.

6: Danger. When faced with imminent danger, fear and the fight or flight instinct, notice the wide range of thoughts and feelings triggered. Using a few keywords, describe what you went through in dangerous situations.

7: Death. When a pet or close family member dies the feelings of loss pierces your inner heart. Remember your feelings of grief. Note the quality of your awareness. Recall feelings, thoughts after the death of a loved one or pet. Did you experience a heightened state of awareness? Or was your awareness level the same as always, automatic and habitual?

Like me after my brother died you more than likely experienced some kind of altered state. People, places and things seemed more alive. In the face of adversity you felt more alert. Your emotions, needless to say, were helter-skelter. I felt a range of emotions – fear, terror, anger, guilt, shock, pain, a deep sense of loss, grief, depression etc.

When you live your life on automatic, unconsciously, when you don't choose to be more acutely aware from minute to minute, day to day, you are like a tree in winter. All your leaves have fallen off your branches. You are dormant to the sun's light.

From time to time "negative" events "happen to you." For a brief moment you sprout a small bud from one of your branches. Temporarily you absorb the sun's rays. You are more alive. Before long the cold winter of unconsciousness settles back in and your green bud of acute awareness freezes and dies.

Conscious energy has a different rate of vibration or frequency than unconscious, automatic, habitual energy. You can compare automatic energy to AM radio and conscious energy to FM radio. They are different frequency bands.

For most, generating and attuning to conscious energy is not much of a priority. Give it a sustained try. Use Opus 3 at the beginning of the chapter. Start your day at the very moment you wake up by saying to yourself, "I am completely aware in the here-now." Continue. Persist with this affirmation every minute of every hour of the day. Make being conscious your number one priority and see what happens.

Everything Has a Consciousness

When my son Dane was about five I showed him a quartz crystal. I told him it was alive and had awareness. He looked at me skeptically and said, "It's just a rock." A few years later when he was in third or fourth grade I was helping him with his science homework. The textbook read something like, "Matter is lifeless." I was outraged. Nothing could be further from the truth. According to quantum, non-Newtonian physics, the reality underlying solid "lifeless" matter is mostly made up of space filled with vibrating energies.

In the 1960s Cleve Backster, polygraph expert and owner of the Backster School of Lie Detection, published his research on plants. He measured plant reactions to thoughts, emotions and events by hooking them up to a polygraph. Backster wrote in the International Journal of Parapsychology in 1968, "It seems to indicate some sort of 'primary perception' or consciousness in every living cell." Everything has a consciousness!

To the sensory/physical being who lives mostly unconsciously and habitually, the statement that everything has a consciousness sounds absurd. They tend to be skeptical just like Dane.

At this point in time there seems to be a cultural belief deeply ingrained and rigidly held that rocks and plants are not conscious and alive. The moon, most believe, is a big, lifeless, dead rock hurling through space orbiting the earth. Animals may have a glimmer of life and consciousness but at best they're low on life's totem pole. It appears there's a cultural change going on since dolphins, whales and elephants have been recognized to having a higher-level consciousness than previously believed.

Sensory/physical beings utilized the five senses as mediums of consciousness. Their consciousness range is limited. They tend to automatically assume things are lifeless. After all, their senses, especially sight and touch, report that the wall is hard stuff, lifeless matter.

Additional to self-remembering, choose to be conscious in the here-now. Say to yourself, "I'm completely aware in the here-now." Look, touch, smell, taste and hear as if everything has a consciousness. What do you notice? You may meet with some resistance. Persist. If you start and then a few minutes later discover you've forgotten to see everything as having a consciousness, simply renew your efforts.

If you want to take the next step in evolution or are currently in process of a fundamental change from a sensory/physical being to becoming an energy being, the fact that everything has a consciousness will become more and more apparent to you. You will become more sensitive and intuitive. New levels of consciousness will be revealed.

A rock will not be a lifeless lump of matter. You will feel its vibration and experience its consciousness. You will begin to evaluate yourself and others not by how much money or how many things but by the quality of consciousness.

CONSCIOUSNESS #1

Conscious structured point many-eyed
Penetrating the earth's crusty hide
Bringing sight to deep caves,
Spaces between atomic waves.

Electron-planets in spiral orbit
Inner space stations silently lit
By sun-protons and microscope eyes
Tiny solar system lives — dies.

Geo-logic engrams in rock crystal
Unspeakable memories digest in earth entrails
The minds of Light-Beings fine-tuned
See the answers plainly runed.

Besides the quiet waters of nuclear seas
Balanced beings awaken from a deep freeze
Here the call of transmitting souls
And leave electron-planets through black holes.

Wombs of earthly energy-mothers
Giving birth to energy world brothers
Who bring gifts of Organic Science,
Natural Order Process, and a new age alliance.

Choosing to Be Conscious

"The first stage of the mythological journey – which we have designated the call to adventure – signifies that destiny has summoned the hero and transferred his spiritual center of gravity from within the pale of his society to a zone unknown." The Hero with a Thousand Faces, Joseph Campbell

A client's husband passed away. I saw her plunge into deep grief. Destiny, her husband's death, summoned her, the call to adventure. She entered a time of more acute awareness.

She had an appointment at my office about two weeks after he died. I reminded myself to observe closely her psychological state. I could see the pain in her face yet I saw the light in her eyes. She was more conscious than I had ever seen her before. Now she had an opportunity to choose to be conscious and experience the "zone unknown."

Choosing to renew keen awareness each and every day is not a top priority in our culture. Money, status, fame, success, image, more things and sensory gratification are, by far, much greater priorities. Looking back at my own childhood, I don't recall anyone ever encouraging me to make being conscious a priority or even a possibility.

I encourage you to respond to the call. Make being conscious the most important priority in your life. I know you don't get paid for it. More than likely you won't get a promotion because you choose to be conscious continually day in and day out.

When you enter and live in the "zone unknown" your life is transformed from a mechanical, automatic life into a magical life where events unfold according to some improvisational script. You star in your life movie taking you on an adventure that deep down feels exactly right. It's scary, even terrifying, at times. Often, you're uncomfortable. Your friends may not be your friends any more. You may feel more alone that you ever have before. Still, the inner rewards far outweigh the outer discomfort, although there are doubts along the way. You do feel more alive; the force is truly with you.

My client was more alive than she had been in years despite her grief. She answered the call, at least for a time. She changed her life dramatically taking a three-month sabbatical from work. She made it clear to her employer that she would only work twenty hours a week instead of fifty.

Staying conscious in an unconscious world is no easy task. There are endless distractions that will hypnotize you into unconsciousness again and again. You have to keep reminding yourself to remember, to self-remember – "I am completely aware in the here-now." Each time you renew your awareness you feel more alive, more in the moment.

Choose the conscious way,
Awaken from hypnotic sleep.
Choose every second of every day
To make the evolutionary leap.

Chapter 4
Living Rhythmically

Living Rhythmically day by day
Seems to be a natural way
Of avoiding insane strife
And leading a balanced life.

COSMIC CODE

Light waves travel nowhere
Are everywhere;
Sense the vibrations
Through the time-space
And the human race.
Be the light
You are,
A Cosmic Star.
Time standing still,
Clocks stop,
Stand atop
Of the world.
In the source,
The universal force.
Be the light being,
Limitless seeing
Through people, places, things
Till every cell sings
A chorus of harmony;
Mind-body unite,
Day-night light.

Finding Your Own Rhythm

If you ever have the opportunity to study the ideas and concepts that have influenced different times you will probably find that certain ideas have a very powerful effect. Often one idea can shape events touching the lives of thousands and even millions of people. When an idea points the way to understand how we are in a certain way then the idea can be very useful.

Now, the idea that each of us may have the opportunity of discovering our basic nature, our true structure and function in life, is a particularly useful idea if we are shown how to discover our basic nature. Unfortunately in our society a certain few decide what your basic nature should be. Then they begin imposing their brand of false reality on you, mostly without you even knowing it.

Social, political, economic, scientific etc. pressures arise and begin forcing, controlling, brainwashing and hypnotizing through advertising their particular goals, values and interests. I use the word 'their' in this context meaning the group's force and direction as a whole.

The so-called mass man or woman who has feelings, thoughts, desires and attitudes, etc. begins to lose track of himself/herself as a unique individual entity having life – breathing air, working, playing, crying, suffering, celebrating and so on.

The mass man and woman, more and more, lose the governing

of his or her own life cycle – that period of time from birth (entering this dimension of living energy structures) to death (exiting this dimension of living energy structures).

Who or what begins to govern us then? Those pressure groups as a whole begin to govern us like bureaucratic Frankensteins. They awaken, come to mechanical life and begin regulating the masses who out of ignorance of natural laws of living created the social, political, economic, scientific, medical, military, etc. institutions which have become like so many pits in Dante's inferno.

What then must be done? It is suggested we each start not with the revolution of the monstrous institutions that devour us daily but with ourselves. Returning to first principles again we should each begin the process of finding our basic nature through the finding of our own rhythm.

This is not a declaration of license – everybody should not do whatever they darn well please, that's anarchy, chaos. Instead, it is a declaration of patient effort to gradually discover and work in harmony with oneself yet always in relation to the dynamic environment whose hells have burned many but have prodded few onto glorious heights of knowledge, love and practical skills.

HERE AND NOW

Those lingering years of learning past
A dozen moments it seems, imbedded now
Upon a solid step and I stand fast
Naïve and apathetic; "World I bow."

Above – or possibly below, another stop
Upon another step which singled out
Made firm by constant use of annual crop
A last moment to decide, do not doubt.

And from what knowledge I have gained thus far
Eve' though minute in manner and pale.
I must decide upon my distant star
For all wandering steps will surely fail.

So say I, climb not each step without thought
But choose your way not by what others sought.

Nature Rhythms

How can we begin to find out your own rhythm? Many of the ancient seers, sages and holy men looked to the living symbols in nature for guidance and method. Nature continues to reveal the laws of life to those who are observant enough to uncover her secrets.

When the family takes off on a camping trip to escape the unexpected, trying and nerve twisting pressures of modern city and suburban living, the arms of mother nature are open wide. The soothing sounds of a brook, the gentle breeze through a pine forest, the warm rays of the morning sun are all greetings to the family while making camp in her open arms.

And it is precisely when the family makes camp that the family members can make their first efforts toward learning about rhythm. Nature is always ready to reveal the natural rhythms that are the heartbeat of her continued existence. By using the five senses – seeing, hearing, tasting, smelling and touching – the natural nature rhythms are recorded on the sensitive vibrational field of the mind-psyche-body.

Take a walk to a pond or lake, pick up a stone and hurl it into the water. It creates concentric ripples going out in all directions. Most all of us have done this for fun at one time or another. But how many of us learn something from it which can expand our awareness and understanding and the universe we inhabit?

One simple lesson out of many which can be learned from the concentric ripples of water started in motion by the thrown stone is the lesson of thinking and feeling reactions. Each day we identify with thoughts and feelings. So and so tells us we haven't done the job right or we've failed an important test or we've just been promoted to manager or we've been accepted at a prominent university. All of these are like the thrown stone causing ripples in concentric rings in the water, a kind of chain reaction.

Reactions like oh, god what am I going to do? I'm quitting: now I'm on top of the world and nobody can stop me; it won't be long and I'll be the best in college, etc. These are just a miniscule few of the concentric rings reactions that ripple through our lives resulting in various happenings, meetings, problems, sorrows, joys, etc.

Nature is rich in rhythms like the water wavelets that can teach us about our daily activities. We don't have to go back to nature or become pantheists but we can learn a lesson or two from mother nature while on a camping trip or walking through a city park which will guide us in living effective, rich and rhythmic lives. What nature rhythms can you discover, learn from and apply to your daily life?

SNOWFLAKES MELTING ON A FIERY ALTAR

A Sunday cheese omelet
And five cups of black coffee.
Warm sun, red leaves.

Strolling through a campus labyrinth,
I'm home inside myself,
Here among the brick, mortar and brains.
Words drift like windless snowflakes
Through my head and feet.

I touch the present with empathy.
No past regrets,
No fear of the future.
I'm home inside myself
Sitting by the fire
Sipping creative ideas
And energized images.

Rare cathedral moments
Transform my spine into a spire
While windless snowflakes fall
Melting on a fiery altar.

Mechanical Rhythms

All of us are subjected almost constantly to the commands of mechanical rhythms. Old outworn traditional values, ideas, mores, customs, codes, creeds, etc. are, for the most part, the machinery that manufactures mechanical rhythms. Whenever we're thinking, feeling and doing automatically chances are, nine times out of ten, some mechanical rhythm has come into our behavior and talked us, thought us, felt us, did us. We are not naturally rhythmic. We are not functioning from out of our own natural rhythm.

Too many mechanical rhythms in our life-field (our pattern of thoughts, feelings, actions, etc.) builds up resistance, blockages and inhibitions against our natural life rhythm. These blockages become like embedded stains in our favorite linen tablecloth – they're practically impossible to get out.

It takes constant and consistent effort finding your own natural rhythm in order to remove the blockages of mechanical rhythms in our life-fields. One way of beginning this effort is to look neutrally and with new eyes at the life you're now living. It's suggested you only look at one area of your life at a time, keeping it down to a few minutes and then building up to fifteen minutes to a half hour.

I've heard of and met business people who after ten, twenty, even thirty years of the rat race sat down one day, took a good look at their self-destructive life-ways and decided to stop. Most take off for the country, go back to nature or move to a warm sunny climate where they can get away from it all.

This is a drastic reaction to a difficult situation filled with negative mechanical rhythms. Perhaps it is the best way for some but most of us cannot take off for the slow-paced country life. Most of the people of the world live in and around metropolitan areas. Many must learn to cope with the rat race or be eaten alive by the self-destructive ways of so-called modern life. Most of us cannot afford to run for our lives. We must make a stand, learn to cope, and act accordingly.

Beginning to look with a cool head for a short time at our life-ways seems to be a more practical approach. In this way we can at least run to the park, observe some of nature's rhythms, learn from them and then apply them to our difficult and different life situations. Then, possibly, strides can be made to live rhythmically even within the mechanical activity of city and suburban life.

The starting of a car, the drone of a crane, the turning of a washing machine, the hard clacking of a jackhammer is the audible cacophony of the machines and their mechanical rhythms. There's an old saying what you worship you become. If we continue to worship the machine – the automobile, the computer, the jet – we will become more like machines and robots. Our automatic mechanical rhythms will be observed by insane power-hungry tyrants who will know what buttons to push in order to get the desired mechanical reaction he needs to maintain his crazed power craving.

Looking at mechanical rhythms from this viewpoint we are left with no choice but to change. Each must find his or her natural rhythm and leave the machine's mechanical rhythms – which are so necessary for modern life – to their unnatural rhythms.

Modern Rush

Some years ago a friend of mine told me an experience which he had involving modern rush. He was very much into snow skiing. One early Saturday morning he hurriedly readied himself gathering all his equipment, skis, poles, boots etc., climbed into the car and drove off heading for the slopes. As he told me, he was very much in a hurry. He couldn't wait to get on the mountain.

Wanting to arrive just when the ski area opened, he exceeded the speed limit and took every short cut he knew. Just a half mile away from his destination he glanced at his watch – five minutes until opening. He felt very self-satisfied that he had made such good time. Turning into the parking lot he pressed down on the gas pedal. The car hit an icy patch, spun around and went into a snowdrift crashing into a sign. He spent most of the day getting the car out of the drift.

There was really no reason for him to rush. He had the day off to do as he pleased. But modern rush, trying to do too much in too short a time, has become a habit with many. How often we hear the phrases I'm late, I've got to run, or hurry up. When we rush, especially for no reason at all like my skier friend, we lose our sense of rhythm. We inflict ourselves unknowingly with blights upon our sensitive nervous system. All of us have seen people who are always rushing helter-skelter. They're shaky, jittery and nervous. Modern rush has become for them a nerve gas, a poison, a plague.

What happens in a very real sense when we lose our natural rhythm and start rushing, rush to get dressed, rush to eat, rush to work, rush while we work, rush to go home, etc., is that we overload the nervous system like an overloaded electrical circuit. The result is a blown fuse and in the long run one suffers a nervous breakdown.

In order to reduce suffering, insanity and other nervous diseases each has to find his or her natural rhythm – as natural and individual as their fingerprints, voice pattern and brain wave – and live by it as much as possible.

The rush hour is part of daily life for many if not most. It is possible to handle rush hour situations intelligently by giving yourself plenty of time plus extra time for the unexpected traffic jam or flat tire, etc. When in a rush hour situations, imagine yourself in the eye of a hurricane where it's clear, calm and quiet yet all around you the winds of rush are churning and swirling. This will help preserve a feeling of calm.

I worked for a New York City department store one Christmas season. A fellow employee, a man in his mid-fifties, used to tell me to "take your time" tying boxes. Even though the lines were twenty or thirty people long and the shoppers snarled and barked for him to hurry, he maintained a rhythm within the rush – like the eye of the hurricane. This method of handling rush is particularly useful in emergency situations to protect oneself from panic, terror, fear, hysteria, etc., all various rushes of force on the nerves which tend to paralyze, blind and cripple.

Hopefully. and with some sensitive intelligence on the part of our leaders, we'll begin to re-examine the structure of our nation's daily schedule. As we begin to see the value of living rhythmically and avoid rush whenever possible we will order and structure our workday differently. Now we rush to work, work all morning, take a half-hour or hour lunch (usually rushed), work all afternoon and rush home at 5 or 6.

Maybe we can take a lesson from the Latinos by taking more afternoon time for a rest, a siesta. The revitalizing of the nerve force in rest or sleep is like a recharging of a battery. The benefit to our society economically, socially, artistically, medically, etc. would be marked.

Balancing the rushed activity of work with quiet relaxing rest or siesta would aid each in finding and following his or her natural rhythm. But, as it stands now, we drain ourselves to the point of exhaustion and unnecessarily so.

BUFFALO BIIL (4TH Grade)

Buffalo Bill was kind and good
He liked to help all people.
He liked to hunt the buffalo.
He knew and loved the trails.
He liked to be an army scout,
To help his country out.
When he was old, he told the young
The adventures he had when he was young.

Rhythmic Alternation

Listening to the song of a bird, watching the rising and setting of the sun or touching the knit weave of a scarf, speak of what has often been called heaven's first law, rhythmic alternation. The ups and downs of joy and sorrow, hardship and happiness, love and hate are poles of the life activity battery. Without the ever-alternating rhythm between positive and negative life loses its vitality. It takes the rubbing, the friction, the conflict to ignite the fires of action, thought and feeling which eventually manifests as events.

In most areas of our lifestyle today we witness the alternation between opposites from the simple example of leaving home in the morning to returning at night, to the more complex national and international alternation between war and peace. In all our institutions: business, government, medicine, home, media, military, arts, agriculture and education, rhythmic alternation takes place whether we are aware of it or not. Just as the microscopic atom maintains its delicate structure because of the dynamic balance of forces between the electrons and the protons so do our institutions survive as long as they maintain some kind of balance between ups and downs, progress and retrogression.

Unfortunately, we do not thoroughly understand and apply the principle of rhythmic alternation to our institutions. When we become over-attached, focused or preoccupied with the positive ups and negative downs, we tend to lose our equilibrium. All of us have, at one time or other, lost our footing while climbing a stairway. Usually we're overjoyed about something, depressed, in a hurry or intoxicated. We lose our balance momentarily and, in that instant, the possibility of injury is increased.

Even the athlete who for only a second loses his or her balance, timing, rhythm risks the possibility of defeat. The musician, who, playing a solo for a philharmonic orchestra, loses his or her rhythm and plays off key spoils the mood and tone of the entire piece. And when we fail to apply rhythmic alternation to our institutions they begin to crumble.

The lesson we need to learn from the natural law of rhythmic alternation is threefold. One, we must see and then know that all life is rhythmic. Two, we must observe ourselves and see where we are not rhythmic. Number three, we must try to find our natural rhythm so that we don't injure ourselves physically, psychologically and/or spiritually. Number three is perhaps the most important of all since without some change in ourselves as individuals there is little chance of change in the social fabric, including our institutions.

A conscious effort toward living rhythmically must include watching how we channel our life energy. There are four basic areas where our energy is channeled: intellectual, feeling, physical and desire. None of these are "pure" channels; they each intermingle with the other. But if we can determine which areas we channel most of our energy, we can attempt to consciously alternate and channel our energy in another complementary direction.

For example, if you have an active intellect, you can balance by participating in some physical activity where you're more into the body instead of words and ideas. Or, if you're too much into feeling, love, the arts and music, you might balance by acknowledging your desires, drives for useful possessions, food and pleasures.

Living more in harmony with nature, human structures and the cosmos by functioning according to the law of rhythmic alternation, the horizons of the future open like fields of wild spring flowers. But if we remain not rhythmic, becoming fixated to one pole or another, we lose our footing and trip up in some unlikely way.

Measured Motion

Anyone who has done any cooking must have noticed the attention they had to pay to measurements. When baking a cake with flour, shortening, sugar, etc. or simply adding salt or pepper to eggs you have to measure your ingredients. If the measurements are not precise the flavor is off and the dish is not tasty. Have you ever noticed the reaction people have to food that hasn't been cooked according to measurement, either overcooked or undercooked, too much of some ingredient or too little of some ingredient?

Every area of our daily lives is dependent on measured motion – rhythms that are precise and proportioned. When we fail to measure our activities in daily life, minor and major crises begin to occur. And when they happened we may think, God, what did I do to deserve this punishment? This or that piece of "bad luck" is nothing more than your own, or someone's lack of precise measurement.

A builder friend who owned his own construction company in the Midwest once told me of an almost tragic incident involving one of his homes. He had a good reputation for building well-designed and constructed homes. He was meticulous about everything from plumbing and heating to wallpaper and interior painting. His reputation for quality gave him a certain measure of success.

Every home built by my builder friend he wisely consulted with an engineering firm who would come out and test the soil on the lot where the new home was to be built. By testing the quality of the soil – clay, loam, sand, black dirt, etc. - they could determine fairly accurately the amount of weight it could withstand without settling.

Anyway, on one particular lot the engineering firm's measurement did not give a true indication of possible excessive settling. My builder friend went ahead and built the house but when the spring rains came the water seeped down along the foundation and into the clay soil below. The foundation on one corner of the house began to sink ever so slightly yet noticeably.

Now here is an example of inaccurate measurement leading to a possible disaster. Fortunately for the builder he did not have to tear down the expensive home and start over. He was able to dig out around the sinking foundation corner and fill in, jack up and secure the corner. But it could have been a lot worse. Suppose some family bought the house and moved in and the house collapsed. Lives could have been lost and the builder could go out of business and perhaps experience feelings of guilt.

In a way, our everyday life can be compared to a building. If our actions, our thoughts, our feelings in relation to the surrounding environment are not measured the house of our daily lives will collapse. Look back for a minute or two at a crisis in your life or in someone else's and see if a lack of measured motion wasn't a good part of the problem. The accident caused by not measuring the amount of alcohol. The disease caused by not eating, sleeping, washing, etc. properly. The lack of money to pay the bills is caused by not sticking to a budget resulting from not using measured arithmetic.

The Greek philosopher, Plato, is quoted as saying, "by measurement is the soul saved." If we substitute the words life energy for soul we have, "by measurement is life energy saved." As we begin to consciously measure our motions, whether thoughts, feelings or actions, we save precious life energy which can be utilized to enhance our life pattern with creative hobbies, contemplations, meditation, observation and experiment. The rewards for following and living daily life according to the law of rhythm and measured motion are many.

Body Rhythms

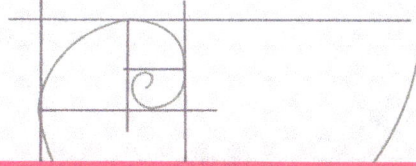

Perhaps the most immediate of rhythmic activities in our daily lives is body rhythms. Not one of us can deny the necessity of rhythmic breathing – in-breath alternating with the out-breath from the first cry at birth to the last gasp at death. Each inhalation brings to the body cells necessary oxygen while each exhalation eliminates toxic carbon dioxide.

The heart also beats out a rhythm. A constant pumping action maintains a flow of blood throughout the circulatory system. The heart beats faster when we are over-anxious, nervous or after vigorous exercise and beats slower while resting, sleeping or meditating. Other body rhythms include hunger, elimination, temperature and sleep, all of which must be paid attention to, otherwise pain, disease and famine are on the prowl.

Another body rhythm little understood is the rhythmic expansion and contraction of the muscles in movement. So often the emphasis in physical education classes and athletic programs is the strengthening and building of the muscles. American football is an example of a sport that values muscle strength.

I recall my own experience in high school when the football coach advised us to get into shape by weight training. It was believed that if we increased the size of our muscles somehow, we would be in a better shape. How far from the truth this was when it came to muscle flexibility. Naturally the weight lifting increased our brute strength but at the same time it reduced the flexibility of muscular movement and tended to crystalize the muscles into patterns that waste great amounts of precious life energy.

Muscle building exercises should be complimented and balanced by muscle flexibility exercises. During football practice each day we would, through a series of exercises, increase our muscular strength as well as loosen up a bit. A fellow player holding his hands on your forehead as you lay on the ground did one exercise that increased the muscle tone in the neck. Next, as you lifted your head, he would hold your head down. This was repeated a number of times.

Now in order to follow a natural rhythm we should have balanced this muscle building exercise with this muscle flexibility exercise: move the head ever so slowly while lying on the ground or floor – so slowly that it seems as though it hardly moves at all. First, roll to the left, then back to the right and back again. This should be repeated at least three times followed by three or four deep, long, quiet breaths.

This is just one example of balancing muscles building with muscle flexibility. If we would apply this simple rhythmic principle to our athletic programs our athletes in all sports from football to swimming would be of a higher quality and greater ability. Even now so-called natural athletes practice muscular rhythm without even knowing it.

One-sidedness

One of the greatest causes of insanity today is one-sidedness. All too often, and without any second thought, we funnel our energies into limited spectrums of thought, feeling and action. We tend to become completely preoccupied with our work, family, sex life or something or other. The result: we forfeit a stable equilibrium in everyday life.

There's a cliché phrase often used to describe one-sided people – all work and no play makes Jack (Jill) a dull boy (girl). When we spend most all of our time, energy and effort on one thing we indeed tend to become a bore. It's like eating bread and water for every meal – you've stayed alive but there's no variety of fruit and vegetables to add a little flavor.

There's nothing duller than to go to a social gathering where a lot of one-sided people are milling around. The doctor knows about doctoring, the accountant knows about accounting, the office worker knows about word-processing. Just about all there is in common are the time, place, food and drink. Meaningless words, gestures and experiences dart, float and drop throughout the room. The wine of meaning has gone bad. Jack and Jill are not only dull but also psychologically one-sided in the sense that the richness, variety and depth of life's possibilities have not touched them.

I'm reminded of a Danish family I stayed with in Copenhagen.

The father in particular surprised me with his fullness of life interests. He was an engineer on the Danish railroad. I had been conditioned to expect all railroad engineers to be like the fictional Casey Jones coming in on track 11, a kind of down to earth good guy who was a hard driving, on time engineer and that's it. My Danish friend was far from one-sided. He spoke five languages, played the piano, read extensively, traveled all over Europe and had a wonderful family among other things. Having a wide range of interests, he was a joy to talk with. I kept imagining him having bull sessions with the conductors in the caboose on the pitfalls of existentialism.

The point is, in part, it's all well and good to specialize; in fact, it's necessary to the social structure to have expert carpenters, masons, engineers, teachers, etc. But without a blending of other life interests the specialty becomes a curse. We lack a fullness of life that brings greater meaning to our primary focus.

The danger of one-sidedness applies as much to groups, organizations, institutions and nations as to individuals. An entire nation can become one-sided in their goals, drives and interests. As the Greeks knew over two thousand years ago, unbalanced forces perish in the void. When we're one-sided for too long, we risk the danger of becoming unbalanced, un-sane. Nazi Germany fell, Rome fell, and other nations have gone to disaster and destruction because they became one-sided in their goals, drives and interests.

THE WAY OF WISDOM #4

Do not go too far
In any one direction
Then your inner fire
Will never face extinction.

Do what must be done
But never more than needed
Then your inner fire
Will never be over heated.

Measure each step taken
Morning, noon and night
Lest you be forsaken
By the ever present light.

Use the eyes, the mind
To see what must be done
Then you will find
The Shining One.

Balance is an art
Practice day-in and day-out
It leads to the golden heart
This is Wisdom's Way.

On Routine and Boredom

In the technological jungle of mass media, mass transportation, mass religion, etc. the signs of sluggish routine and weighty boredom are everywhere to be seen. The very word mass describes the inertia involved in most all of our institutions especially the religious and the government. Government and religion often cling obsessively to the past.

Which one of us has not gone to some government agency like the IRS (Internal Revenue Service), DMV (Department of Motor Vehicles), etc. and had to wait in numerous lines, go through endless red tape and come out a nervous wreck. The government employee seems extremely machine-like, suffering from acute routine and boredom. They suffer from un-rhythmic weakness, an unbalanced and unconscious activity. This is not only true with government employees but workers in various other industries as well.

Which one of us has not felt some loss of rhythm in the religious arena? The religious institutions no longer, for the most part, raise the energy level. Instead, the quality of its member's energy lowers many into a quagmire of drowsy boredom.

The loss of meaning in a religious practice is partly to blame but much can be attributed to the outworn non-functional principles – dogma – adhered to which are often anti-natural order and false to life facts. When we stubbornly cling to past ways and methods and violate our own structure and function in life's plan, we suffer the consequences by losing our rhythm - routine activity follows, then boredom, eventually depression and finally psychological and/or physical disease.

Perhaps a story will illustrate the point.

On a faraway planet called Errornot lived a lonely suffering man name Zotar. Nothing had life for him. Even as he ate he tasted nothing. Everything had lost its flavor. He was bored to death; in fact, he wanted to dive off the cliff of no return. He would have except that he was too bored and depressed to get up the energy to jump.

The inhabitants of Errornot were a sensitive people especially those who lived in the countryside of Borg. They lived in rhythmic harmony with the stars, trees and streams. Because of their sensitivity they could detect easily a loss of rhythm in another even at great distances. They began to feel the weightiness of Zotar's boredom and in order to avoid a plague of boredom in Borg decided to help Zotar find his rhythm.

Two Borgians coated in bee honey to protect them from picking up Zotar's boredom went out and brought Zotar to the town of Borg. Everybody acted as if they were bored to death - moaning, groaning and imitating Zotar's suffering. Zotar realized what boredom was. He began to find his rhythm again and the people of Borg laughed over their successful trick.

As the story suggests by becoming aware of our lack of rhythm we take the first step toward regaining our natural rhythm. When we're bored and live routinely, our energy has gotten stuck in the cement of rigid concepts, feelings and desires. Perhaps at that point one of our only choices is to find or come across others who live more harmoniously so that we can recover completely from weighty boredom and rigid routine.

Mental Rhythm

Of all the areas of life where we channel our energies the mental realm, more than most, needs rhythmic activity. Especially in the last two hundred years with the industrial revolution, scientific materialism and the digital jungle, the emphasis on the mental function of analysis – separation, breaking down into parts – has carried the prime emphasis in our educational systems, particularly in the United States. The rhythmic complementary mental function of synthesis – blending, combining, joining, bringing together – is little used, little know and practically ignored. The end result of too much analysis without a rhythmic change to synthesis is narrow-mindedness, over specialization, verbal arguments and war.

A story told by the Buddha to his disciples tells what usually happens when a mental rhythm between analysis and synthesis is missing. Raja Savatthi ordered a man to assemble all the blind subjects of the kingdom and bring an elephant before them. Then the man said to the assembled group, "This is an elephant." He permitted one to feel the elephant's head, another its ear, still another its tusk and so on until the trunk, foot, back, tail and tuft were covered. To each blind subject, the man said, "This is an elephant."

Finally the Raja turned to his blind subjects and asked them, one by one, what they thought an elephant was. The one who felt the head thought an elephant was a pot. The ear feeler was sure it was a winnowing basket. The tusk was thought to be a plowshare, the trunk a plow, the foot a pillar, the tail a whip and the tuft a floor duster. And they quarreled, shouting, "I know what an elephant is." "No, I do." "You're wrong, this is what it is." They began to wrestle and fight. The Raja was pleased, for he had made his point.

The blind subjects each touched a part of the whole. Analysis deals with the parts. Without synthesis – bringing together of disunited parts – seeing the whole, quarreling and warfare are practically inevitable.

I first began to discover this problem while going to the university. Each department whether history, English, physics, etc. took its department to be a clear-cut entity by itself. One semester I decided to take a course on Ancient Greece from three different departments and see what would happen. From the history department I took Greek history, from the philosophy department I signed up for a Greek philosophy class and from the humanities department I signed up for Greek religions.

Needless to say, I had three different professors who assigned similar reading lists but who had quite differing viewpoints. On the exams I answered very similar questions in almost the same way and would invariably get it marked incorrect or correct depending on the view of the teacher. This is when I began to see that there was no such thing as right and wrong, only someone's personal analytical opinion. Right and wrong, true and false, good and bad were the dichotomies of the analytical dividing function. By studying Ancient Greece synthetically, as well as analytically, I saw more of a whole picture which was neither true or false, right or wrong but a growing awareness of the Ancient Greek lifestyle.

Mental rhythm between separation and bringing together is absolutely necessary to the health of the individual and the stability of civilization. Isidore Friedman said it well in Organics: The Law of the Breathing Spiral: "In a deeper sense, analysis-synthesis are two phases of the same process, and in actual life, can never be separated. To use analysis only in solving daily problems or synthesis only is like trying to breathe in only or wanting to only breathe out solely. From this kind of procedure can only come chaos and destruction (de-structuring) and paralysis of healthy living and functioning."

Rhythmic Feeling

What exactly is a feeling? All of us have felt good, excited, happy or bad, depressed and sad. Using the analogy of a radio, we can define a feeling relatively accurately and scientifically. Go to your radio, turn it on and set the dial to your favorite station. Maybe rock, soul, country western, classical, jazz, etc. happens to be your particular sound. Now the music you're listening to can be compared to a feeling that you're experiencing at any given time. If you turn the dial to another station you'll more than likely hear some other kind of music. When we find ourselves in some other situation (change the station frequency) we're liable to have a different feeling. Basically, then, a feeling is a frequency of energy registered by the psycho-physical organism and reacted to by the mental-emotional faculties.

There is a big difference between thinking and feeling, although they are as intimately connected as hydrogen and oxygen in a water molecule. So often in daily conversation, on talk shows and in the print media, the two words are inadvertently used to mean the same thing. More times than I can count I've heard someone ask another, "What do you think of such an such?" Often, they respond by saying, "I feel such and such." Or it's turned around. The question is, "How do you feel about such and such?" And the answer will begin with the words, "I think." This unconscious confusing of two entirely different aspects of the human experience seems innocent enough on the surface but if we confuse these two in greater issues where lives are at stake, there is nothing innocent about it; the difference is para-mount. Thinking involves activity of the mental centers in comparing, contrasting and weighing observable facts while feeling is a kind of 'inner' sensation registered passively.

Now that we've clarified to some degree what a feeling is we need to discover what our particular range of feelings are so that we can bring a natural alternating rhythm to the realm of feelings. If you have ever spent a day at the beach watching the steady rise and fall of the surf and the changing hues of grey, blue, brown, green and white in the water, you have seen in nature a parallel to the natural rhythm that our feelings should follow if not repressed.

There's an excellent way of becoming more aware of our feeling states so that we can maintain a more natural flow. Buy some 3 X 5 notecards. Be sure to write the date on each card. Keep them handy throughout the day, by your bedside in the morning and in your pock-et or purse through the work-a-day hours. Every hour on the hour, as your circumstances permit, stop and ask yourself, how do I feel? Take your time. Determine your feeling state the best you can and write it down on the notecard. Choose a couple of keywords that describe it best. Repeat this each hour throughout the day for at least two weeks. By doing this exercise you can get a fairly accurate map of where your feelings are focused.

Knowing this to some extent, you can start to consciously restore balance to your feelings. For example, if you find yourself de-pressed to a great extent you can decide to seek out activities and situ-ations that give you feelings of joy and pleasure. On the other hand, if you find yourself overly positive you can balance by finding activities or situations, which quiet you down. By finding your own rhythm in feeling you balance your feeling energies leading to a more wholesome and healthy everyday life

The Principle of Least Resistance

As we go about our daily duties and chores fulfilling resposibilities and obligations we must avoid as much as possible every stress and strain. When our thinking and feeling become more rhythmic our actions must follow less we throw ourselves off balance again. By putting into practice the principle of least resistance we gain great economy of time and energy. When tension builds from over pressure either at home or at work, we should remind ourselves that we've lost our rhythm once again and in order to regain it nothing helps more than following the line of least resistance.

Before taking any action from getting out of bed to washing the dishes, mentally anticipate each act in the process of execution. For example, take getting out of a chair. In order to follow the line of least resistance, first let go of the tension in the stomach, neck and back. Then leaning forward from the hip joint in a swift swiveling motion allows you to stand without clutching every muscle.

Mountain climbers are particularly knowledgeable about economy of action. Some years ago, in the mid-1960s, I had the opportunity to learn mountain climbing in the Grand Tetons of Wyoming. My teacher, Glen Exum, was a mountain man in appearance, reputation and in action.

As a climber at age 60, he was still formidable; something hard to believe until you saw how he climbed.

Most of the young people in my class were in their teens and early twenties; ready and eager to make the ascent. Mr. Exum gathered us together and told us right off that if we wanted to climb we must learn economy of action and rhythmic motion. That didn't make sense to most of us until later on up the trail to the climbing area. As we started up the trail, he suggested we walk deliberately picking each spot and stepping firmly, lightly and consciously.

Well, that lasted about 5 minutes. He was too slow for us. Instead, we all raced right by him, telling him we'd meet him at the base of the mountain. Before we were three-quarters of the way, we stopped to rest. We were already exhausted. After a few minutes, Mr. Exum, with a smile on his face and his gait steady and rhythmic, hiked on by us.

As a climber, Mr. Exum was a master of the principle of least resistance. Despite his years, he could hike and climb for hours without a rest because he did not waste energy rushing, wanting to get to the summit all at once. Just as diligently as Mr. Exum conserved his energy in climbing, we all must conserve out energy throughout our day whether climbing stairs or writing a letter. In this way we cultivate rhythmic living.

A couple of aides to learning and establishing economy in the use of your energy include singing, humming and breathing. While you work keep time by singing or humming. Also, when out walking inhale slowly and steadily as you take six steps, then hold the breath as you pace three steps; then exhale gradually as you pace six steps, hold bated breath while you pace three steps, etc. You can increase or decrease the number of steps until you find the count that is easiest, but always concentrating on the rhythm.

By applying the principle of least resistance to simple daily activities, we gain our natural rhythm as well as extra energy so valuable and necessary if we desire to fulfill our potential during our short stay on this earth.

Conscious Attention – Subconscious Retention

Next time you're at the local supermarket or department store take time out from your shopping and watch how other shoppers observe, look, examine the products they're considering buying. They pick the merchandise up, feel it, weigh it, size it up, search for imperfections and look for the good points. It's amazing to watch this happen especially since once they decide for or against their attention disappears. Their momentary conscious attention – a keen awareness of what is happening in the outer environment and in their thoughts, feelings and actions – is usually not carried over into the next activity. If it were, their opportunities in life would be expanded a thousand-fold.

Now when we use our conscious attention, like the shoppers in the store, in other areas of life such as in relationships, work, inner development, etc. the subconscious becomes fertile with possibilities. Basically, there's a pumping cycle between what we take in consciously and what is retained subconsciously. When we make a focused effort to be consciously attentive, the subconscious retains the impression more clearly and exactly. But when we go through our day half out of it, unaware, unconscious the impressions taken in are reflected in the subconscious like into a curved and twisted mirror – everything is misshaped and distorted. The subconscious becomes a distortion of the everyday world much like the funhouse mirrors distort the size and shape of your face and body.

The subconscious is a kind of spectrum of subliminal awareness that retains, stores and recollects facts, data, memories, etc. Naturally, then, when the subconscious is seeded with distortions our facts, data, memories are hazy, deformed and inaccurate. A vicious cycle is set up; our consciousness in daily life feeds distorted impressions to the subconscious which in turn feeds back distorted memories, facts, data, etc.

When two or more unconscious people get together, the probability of disagreement and conflict is practically inevitable. When two diplomats from two nations get together, the possibility of agreement is close to zero despite all the hand shaking, back slapping and verbal chitchat. On the silent nonverbal level there are two people who are unconscious – who do not use conscious attention in their every daily action and so feed the subconscious misconceptions, opinions, hearsay, second hand information, etc. all of which lead to confusion, conflict and chaos.

We must begin practicing conscious attention, when we buy something at the store, while at home, while driving the car or at work. An exercise which is particularly helpful in developing conscious attention is done by placing an object in front of you and then looking at it with bare attention – not thinking, not fantasizing, not analyzing, etc. – just conscious attention. At first, it will, more than likely, be difficult to hold your attention even for one second but with practice and more practice your attention span will increase.

Eventually your conscious attention will be strong enough and sensitive enough to be continued in the most mundane activities. When that stage is reached, the subconscious will be a storehouse of order and structured patterns that reflect the events of daily life faithfully and accurately. Bringing a rhythmic harmony between conscious attention and subconscious retention will act like a dynamo of energy enhancing and enriching your life-pattern.

CHARTER

Lift off, the cabin's solitude
Where strangers sense the space.
And calm, the satisfying mood:
Something like a fulfilling finished chase.

Steady roar forms the background
And exotic delicacies served.
Friendly smiles given by girls in the blue are found,
While wings dip and fuselage curved.

Unseen, hidden behind closed doors,
Hands and minds lead the charter home.
Those diligent control men calculate the course
Making sure temptation escapes the tomb.

Drop the flaps, bend the wings
Toward our destination dark below.
Set down where sturdy wheels cling
To be a part again of avenues that grow.

Musical Rhythms

It is said that the ancient Pythagoreans used music to evoke peaceful feelings and serenity. They believed the human body was a kind of sounding board which responds immediately to the vibratory effects of sound. Good music – music that is pleasant and harmonious – is available through the radio, the phonograph, the smartphone, the Internet and the television. The sounds we hear have definite and specific effects on the physiological organism.

With the advent of the modern technological city, there's been a rapid increase in nervous and psycho-neurotic ailments. Mechanical rhythms began to impose their disturbing effects not only on our nerves but also on our social structure. As it is nature's law to balance every negative with a positive, so it is in the social sphere. The electronic, digital media was birthed at approximately the same time as the mechanical rhythms of the modern city – automobile, machinery of all kinds. However, the music, instead of restoring our natural life rhythm, led us even further from the natural working of the human structure.

The radio and the photograph in the early part of the twentieth century and the television and the Internet in the second half of the twentieth century often brought to the public ear music that featured discordant rhythms, dissonances and exaggerated tempos. In and of themselves jazz, ragtime and blues were not detrimental. Nonetheless, their wild rhythms cried out the agony of mechanical and imposed rules, regulations that violated the natural law of rhythm. The negative effect of the dissonant music was that it did not restore one to a state of harmony and balance but more often than not reinforced the pain, agony, sorrow and suffering caused by the technological unharmonious vibrations.

In recent years the use of music to help bring balance to frayed nerves has been explored. In factories, in department stores, in doctor and dentist offices, music has been used to calm, heal and energize. But we must ask ourselves, what music should be used and perhaps more importantly who is playing the music?

First, what kind of music should be listened to? If we desire to find our natural inner rhythm, it is whatever music will bring stability and balance to our life pattern. For example, if we are sick and diseased, we need to listen to music that is specifically structured to heal and re-store vitality. If we are depressed, we need to listen to music that evokes joy. If we are angry, we need to listen to music that calls forth a mood of peace.

The answer to the second question, who is playing the music, is critical. If the musicians are living an unbalanced and unrhythmic life, all the technical skill in the world cannot aid them in playing truly harmonic music. The musician who lives rhythmically shares his or her harmonious inner state.

It is said that music binds people together. Perhaps scientific yet heartfelt research into the structure and function of music could come up with finding music more appropriate to the structure of human nature than a national anthem or a number one song on the top forty. The fruits of such research would be part of a musician's course of study. He must use and practice them or he cannot be a true rhythmic and harmonious musician.

The Greeks held the science of music in high regard. It is not surprising, therefore, that they legislated to preserve the purity of their music. Composers were fined and even exiled from the state if their compositions were considered to be detrimental to the public good. Let's hope we will not have to legislate. Perhaps the social pressures will increase to the point where when a musician does not assume responsibility for the effects of his music on others he will find little if any work.

THROUGH THE LIGHT-DARK

Magic mystery time
Events glimpse heartbeats
Through the light-dark.
Time frame joy
Purpose destiny happens,
Moving on to the heart
Of the matter.

Biorhythm

In recent years scientists in many countries have been investigating what they call biological clocks, that is, cyclic or rhythmical changes in the human body. Three of these biological clocks have been grouped together into a system call biorhythm. Based on date of birth, a biorhythm chart plots three interrelated cycles – physical (23 days), emotional (28 days) and intellectual (33 days).

The 23-day physical rhythm is believed to originate in the muscular cells and fibers. This cycle affects your physical strength, endurance, energy, resistance and confidence. The 23-day rhythm is divided into two, 11 ½ days is the ascending part of the cycle. Theoretically, these are the days when a person feels a strong physical vitality. Physical work seems easier; athletes perform better; diseases are not as likely to invade the body.

The second half of the 23-day rhythm is referred to as the recharging period. During this 11 ½ days you tend to tire more easily. Despite the reduced strength and endurance, it does not necessarily mean these are "bad" days. It may be a perfect time to be more relaxed, restful and unwind from excessive physical action.

The 28-day emotional rhythm governs the automatic or so called sympathetic nervous system. Again, the cycle is divided into half periods, 14 days each. The first 14 days represents a positive time of increased optimism and cheerfulness. Creative work, romance and cooperation with others are usually favorable during this half cycle.

The second half-cycle represents a recuperative period during which you are more inclined to become over-excitable, irritable and negative. Emotional types will find this 28-day rhythm particularly meaningful.

It's interesting to note that the weekday you were born on will always repeat on the first and on the fifteenth day of the 28-day emotional rhythm. If you were born on a Sunday, for example, then every other Sunday represents a day of emotional flux going from positive to negative or negative to positive.

The 33-day intellectual rhythm has a half-period as well, 16½ days. During the first half thinking tends to be clearer, the memory functions better and mental response is at a peak. It is claimed that students absorb new subjects more easily during this time.

The second 16½ days in the 33-day cycle represents the period when the ability to think is reduced. Students generally will find it more difficult to absorb new subjects. Instead, this is a time conducive to review and to digest previously studied subjects.

Each of the three biorhythm cycles have critical points on the first day and middle point of the period. Critical days, as they are called, are considered switch-point days. In other words, you should be more careful during critical days because you tend to be in a state of flux, which leads to a certain degree of instability. Critical days, it should be pointed out, are not in themselves dangerous. Rather, you should think of them as days when your reactions to certain situations may bring about a critical situation.

Ohmi Raily Way Company, a private bus and railroad firm in Japan, began using biorhythm charts for their drivers and cut back accidents by fifty percent. Every morning the company lists on a bulletin board the various cycles for its four hundred bus drivers showing whether it is going to be a "good" day or "bad" day for each. The drivers who are facing critical days are warned to be more alert to possible shortcomings and to take extra caution to prevent accidents.

Perhaps you will have your biorhythm chart done and test the biorhythm system for yourself.

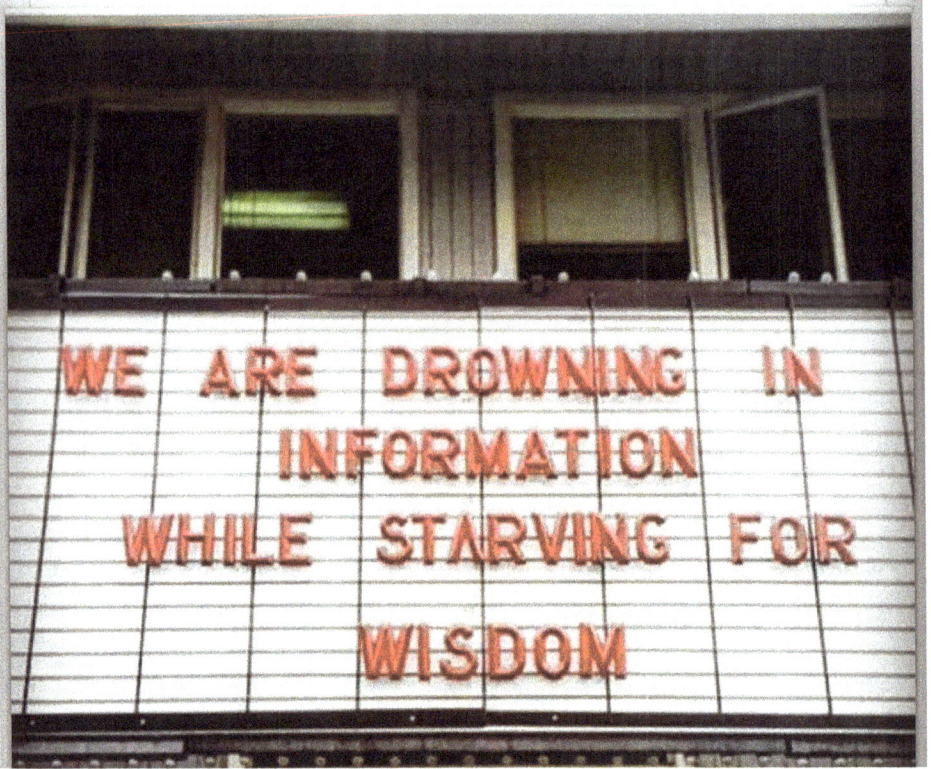

Chapter 5
Whole Living

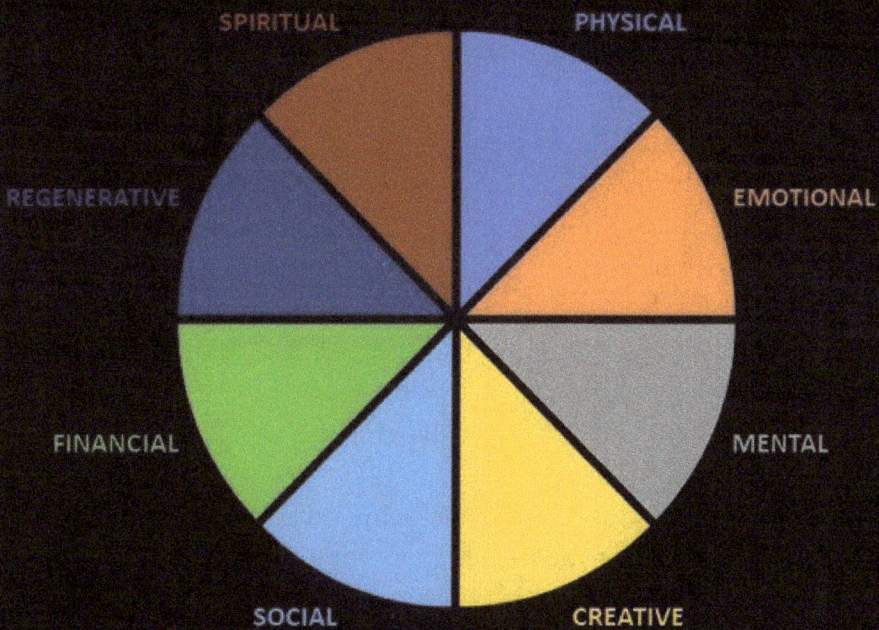

Created by Dane Nielsen

Look around you. Everywhere there are objects – tables, telephones, buildings, sidewalks, food, clothing, etc. On closer inspection of any object you will see that it is made up of many parts. Take a telephone. There is the screen, the dial pad, the microphone, the ringer, the speaker and so on; ordered and interrelated in such a way to make the phone function. Choose an object close to you and see if you can see the parts integrated to make the whole object.

Now look at others and, above all, look at yourself, especially from a psychological viewpoint. How many are integrated in their lifestyle, training, developing and unfolding their entire – whole – being? Basically, there are eight areas of living which if developed and balanced in relation with the others will go a long way toward establishing a pattern of whole living: physical, emotional, mental, creative, relationships, regenerative, financial and spiritual.

Here's a brief list of what falls under each category. The lists are by no means complete but point in a general direction, which, if followed, will widen and develop that area of your being.

Physical: Exercise, relaxation, diet, hygiene.
Emotional: Awareness of moods, taming automatic reactions, practicing non-identification, not getting too excited or too depressed, breaking infantile emotional tendencies, accepting responsibilities for your actions.
Mental: Study, reading, reflection, scientific thinking, planning, structured ideas.
Creative: Hobbies, crafts, dance, music, writing, the creative arts.
Relationships: Social activities, communication, other's needs.
Regenerative: Digesting past experiences, eliminating pressure points of the past, change, transformation of old into the new.
Financial: Means of income, balancing the books, savings, investments, livelihood.
Spiritual: Perception, awareness, being quiet inwardly and outwardly, learning to tune into higher vibrations, self-knowledge, the awakening of inner faculties.

There was a man with a family, a suburban house, a business and many of the other signs of material success. Making money consumed his time and energy like fire consumes wood. Each day at the buzz of the alarm he would spring from his bed and start thinking in dollar signs. How could he swing the big deal? How could he expand his business? How could he make the second million? These were the questions that interested him most.

His family saw neither hide nor hair of him since he left the house early and came home after everyone had eaten dinner. Even Saturday was spent organizing things at the office. The one day each week, Sunday, which was free he spent reading financial papers and magazines. He did not want to be bothered so he'd lock himself in his study most of the day.

Year after year of this went on to the point of obsession. His wife and children saw him more and more not as husband and father but as an unsane money mad businessman who could care less what happened to them. The family became more and more divided. The wife tried to communicate with her husband. Unfortunately, he could not see what she was saying. He dismissed her usually with the words, "Oh, there's nothing the matter. It's all in your imagination."

Not long after her communication attempts she packed a few things and taking the children moved to her home state. The businessman found the note she left but was too narrow minded to realize what he had done blaming his wife for everything. His heart was cold, having little understanding of her reasons for leaving.

After the divorce, the businessman went right on making money, stockpiling millions upon millions of dollars. The rest of his life was a shambles, living like a recluse. No one could get close to him. The financial section of the newspaper was his best friend.

Looking at the wheel of whole living, it's apparent that seven out of eight areas were left uncultivated. The businessman's obsession with the financial robbed the energy from other areas denying him the joy of a balanced, harmonious and integrated lifestyle. He became so absorbed in the money end of things that he could not see or hear anything from outside the dollar realm.

What could this man have done? Using the wheel of whole living, he could easily, in a matter of minutes, realize where most of his time and energy were focused. The steps for using the wheel are as follows. Sit down at a table; place the wheel in front of you on the table. Place your index finger in each of the eight sections beginning with the physical and continuing clockwise all the way around to the spiritual.

While holding your finger on a section, review that area of your life. If little or no energy is being channeled in that area, then in order to live a more integrated life, a more well-rounded life, steps should be taken to fulfill that part of your life.

Now, our businessman friend would find that the financial sector consumed nearly all of his time and energy. He suffered from chronic one-sidedness. Only an eighth of the wheel was active. The remaining 7/8 was left virtually undeveloped. Ideally, we should never become overly active in one, two or three areas but should genuinely strive to be active in all eight.

Naturally, the proportions will change depending upon your particular situation. Perhaps relationships command a lot of attention forcing you to leave out the physical exercise you usually get at the health club. Don't worry. Simply tell yourself that at the earliest possible opportunity you will re-establish your usual exercise routine.

The wheel of whole living is a valuable life-enriching tool. It can be used almost any place at almost any time. Used every day, it will help you steer the course of your day in a wiser direction. Used at least once a week, it will help you balance your energies.

EARTHWALK #1

Calm the thought, feeling, action boil
Plant your life seed in perception's soil.
Awareness of positive-negative brings light
To mind-body, a guiding star in blackest night.

The animal in man hungers, desires
Roasts and burns in hell's fires
Cool your urges, your wants, your craving
Take careful note of now you're behaving.

Lower emotion wants to rule the roost
Give the orders, avoid structure's boost,
You must take charge, be the boss
Otherwise a lighted life is your loss.

Heated speech is automatic mutter
By the higher considered deluded stutter.
Keep the word plain and sane
Unemotional, devoid of suffering and pain.

Do not run around helter-skelter
Your energy level is your shelter.
Make your actions ordered, measured
That will bring what you have treasured.

Chapter 6
How to Stop Automatic Thinking

Fred tossed and turned all night. His mind raced with thought after thought after thought. He had a crucial job interview the next day and he could not stop thinking about it.

Gail was taking a college English class. She kept thinking: 'I've got to do well; I've got to pass. What if I don't know an answer? What am I going to do if I fail?' She was so busy thinking about the exam she didn't give it her full attention.

Harriet was thinking about her handsome husband as she began preparing the evening meal. She picked up the pot roast to put in the pre-heated oven. She was so wrapped up in her daydream that she accidently touched the metal shelf with the side of her hand. Thankfully, it was only a minor burn.

Jack was walking down the street thinking about the big business deal that he just made. He thought about all the money he was going to make and what he would spend it on. Not watching where he was walking, he stepped squarely in a pile of dog poo.

Karen was depressed. Nothing was going right. Confused thoughts rushed in and out of her mind as she sliced an onion. The knife slipped, cutting her finger.

Lenny was climbing the stairs to the train platform. He was thinking about the best-selling novel he was going to read on the way to work. He tripped on a step, fell down and bruised his knee.

Myra was driving to her son's school. She had an appointment with her son's teacher about his grades. She couldn't stop thinking about what the teacher might say. She unintentionally drove through a red light almost causing an accident.

All of these people were caught up in automatic thinking. Millions of men and woman are hooked on the bad habit of automatic thinking. Most do not know they are suffering from the problem. And those who do, do not know how to stop it.

What exactly is automatic thinking? It is the uncontrolled barrage of thoughts, words, images, words, images, memories, ideas, etc., through the mind-brain. It often occurs in the form of daydreams, fantasies, flashbacks, inner talking and critical thinking about others and oneself.

What are some of the negative effects of automatic thinking?

a) Blinds you from seeing What Is
b) Wastes your precious life energy
c) You lose contact with the present situation
d) You unconsciously program your subconscious
e) Makes your ego personality more inflexible
f) You tend to live in the past
g) You often attract negative events
h) You have more difficulty communicating
i) Your senses do not record accurately
j) You tend to react more emotionally
k) You have more difficulty relaxing
l) You suffer from mental and physical fatigue
m) You suffer from insomnia
n) Etc.

The next question is: How can you stop (slow down) automatic thinking? First, you must become aware of when you are thinking automatically. Begin observing yourself morning, noon and night. Catch yourself when you start unconscious, automatic thinking.
Ask yourself when you catch a train of thought: Why am I thinking?

Perhaps you are only wasting time and energy. Perhaps there is no rhyme or reason for you to be thinking.

Now ask yourself: When you want are you able to stop (slow down) thinking with ease? If the answer is no, then you must make a firm decision to learn how to stop automatic thinking. No doubt it will be an up and down process of successes and failures. But, if you persist in taking specific action, you'll be able to turn off the thinking at will.

Gradually you must detach from all automatic thinking frequencies. Uncontrolled thoughts, words, images, memories, ideas, etc. are vibrations that cause a kind of static in the mind-brain-nervous system. Intense identification with these negative mental vibrations leads to the pernicious habit of automatic thinking.

One way of detaching from automatic thought frequencies is with rhythmic breathing. Sit or lie down and get as comfortable as possible. As gently as you can, breath through the nostrils. Inhale slowly and deeply saying to yourself, PEACE. Then exhale slowly and completely saying to yourself, QUIET.

Also, you can try conscious sensory awareness. Look at everything and everyone around you. Notice the colors, shapes, designs, textures, etc. Listen to the sounds, tones, noises, etc. Smell the odors, aromas, scents, etc.

If you catch yourself slipping back into automatic thinking, persist with conscious sensory awareness. Take a walk observing nature's handiwork: the trees, the flowers, sky, etc. Do not allow your thoughts to wander from the present moment – THE NOW.
In order to break the habit of chronic identification with automatic thoughts, practice bare attention. Bare attention is looking without association. Do not form any opinions, judgments and/or beliefs about anything or anyone. Simply look without association.

Another preventive measure is the practice of self-remembering. As often as possible throughout the day, say silently, I (YOUR NAME) am completely aware in the here-now. Whenever you catch yourself indulging in excessive thinking, go into self-remembering. Practicing bare attention and self-remembering on a regular basis will sharpen and refine your conscious focus. Both skills will go a long way toward developing you into a conscious thinker. Conscious thinking rests on a foundation of accurate sensory awareness and acute present attention.

Stopping (slowing down) automatic thinking also involves learning how to relax. If the mind is full of uncontrolled thoughts then the body is more than likely full of excess tensions. Relaxing is one of the most efficient ways of halting a Niagara of thought.

Be Yourself – the Art of Relaxation by Israel Regardie is an excellent guide to relaxation. This book is out of print. It is available as a PDF on Patreon as is Annie Payson Call's Power Through Repose (Patreon.com/spiritualfrequencies). These books are a treasure trove of relaxation methods.

One final key: when you wake up in the morning, become keenly and immediately aware of your automatic thinking. Take steps to stop it before you lock into it unconsciously. Your early morning efforts each day will reap unexpected rewards throughout the day.

Once you are free of the grip of automatic thinking, you will experience life on whole new frequency band. Everything will become clearer and simpler. You will enjoy what you like even more. And what you don't like will seem less repulsive.

Chapter 7
How to Change Your Life from Inside

The power is ours to make or mar
Our fate on the earliest morn,
The darkness and the radiance are
Creatures within the spirit born
Yet, bathed in gloom too long, we might
Forget how we imagined light.

Colton

Your inner level of consciousness
Or awareness determines your
Outer conditions. To change your
Outer world, change your inner
World.

Vernon Howard

Irv was in his early forties, moderately successful with a wife and two teenage sons. Viewing Irv's life from the outside, most would conclude that things were going well for him. This "going well", as it turns out, was only an appearance. Inside, Irv was restless, dissatisfied and eager for some stimulating change.

When he daydreamed, or chewed the fat with his buddies, adventurous thoughts buzzed in his mind. He fanaticized an exotic affair with a Polynesian beauty. He believed if he moved to California happiness would be his the rest of his days.

At other times, he considered finding a new job or starting his own business. In his wildest thoughts he considered taking up skydiving or racecar driving.

Somewhere along the line Irv's zest for living dramatically diminished. Still, he was an expert at keeping up the front. He said the right things, did the right things and smiled at the right time.

Eventually, Irv's inner dissatisfaction reached a nadir. He wanted out. He had to do something.

He startled his wife by asking for a separation. In the next breath, he said he was quitting his job.

Now, she was shocked. She believed Irv's front. She never suspected his discontent.

Clearly, Irv needed a change. Unfortunately, he attempted to change by changing conditions on the outside. True change is rarely accomplished this way.

Vernon Howard writes: "Nothing is added to us when we merely change a residence, profession or spouse. It is like a man stranded on a lonely island who seeks self-betterment by moving his camp to the opposite side of the island. The scenery may be different, but he is still as stranded. We all sense this, but do not know enough about genuine deliverance in self-change."

As it turned out, Irv was even more miserable after the separation. Quitting his job didn't help either. Irv needed to change, but he did not know how to go about it.

Lasting change comes about by changing the way you think, feel and act. Scientific investigation confirms this statement.

In recent years biofeedback instruments have been used in training people to control some of their body's inner workings.

The Hour Glass of Change

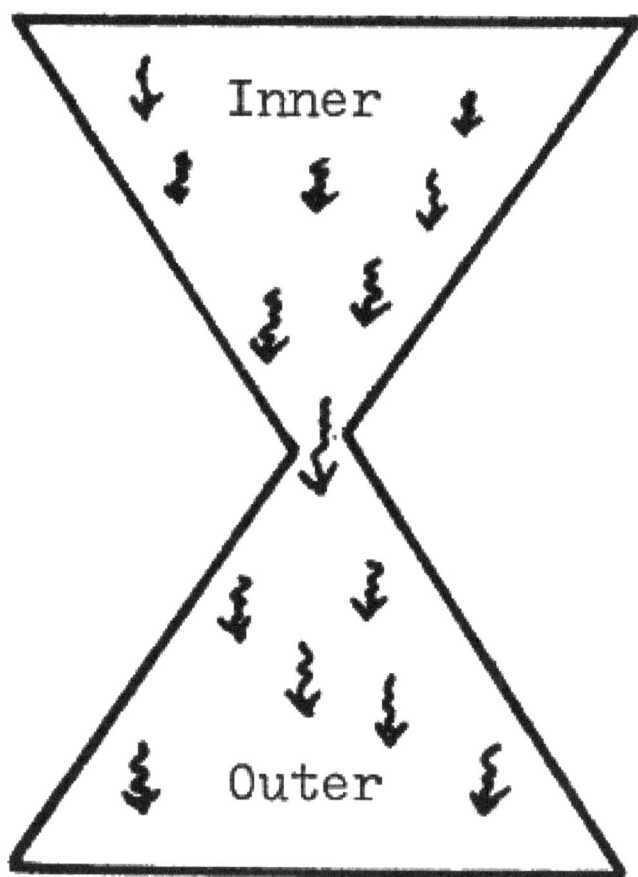

Biofeedback equipment measures the body's activities – heart rate, blood pressure, temperature, muscle contractions and brain waves. By altering thought, feeling, mood and image the patient is able to better regulate some of the body functions.

Dr. Alyce Green of the Menninger Foundation says: "The person visualizes and feels the desired change that will influence the meter and allows the body to carry out the instruction. The feeling seems to be the instruction."

This feeling has been reported by many successful performers to be, at least in the early stages of learning, a composite image, emotion and body sensation, but after a skill is thoroughly learned, the body sensation can be 'turned on' at will, often with no need for any particular mental image or emotion.

Often biofeedback is not needed for more than a few weeks. Most important, biofeedback is not addictive because voluntary internal control is established, rather than dependence on an external agency.

Irv needed to change from inside, psychologically. Yet, the principle is the same: change the way you think and feel and you change your life from inside.

The relationship between inner-outer must be made crystal clear. When your thoughts are positive and you feel good, people and events will reflect those constructive thoughts and feelings. Depressed thoughts and feelings will attract depressing people and events.

Realize your thoughts and feelings are vibrations, which not only affect your body (measured by biofeedback) but also affect the kind of people you spend time with and the kind of situations you attract.

Look at the Hour Glass of Change (page 100). The squiggly arrows in the upper (inner) triangle symbolize thoughts, feelings, moods, desire, images, concepts, emotions and the like. The squiggly arrows in the lower (outer) triangle represent events, people, situations, jobs, environments and so on.

To establish the definite connection between inner-outer for yourself, perform the following experiment. Upon rising in the morning, think only of beauty. Fill your mind exclusively with thoughts of beauty for the first hour of the day. What do you notice? Record your findings so that you can compare your observations with the next part of the experiment.

As soon as possible, preferably the following morning, wake up and begin thinking of ugliness. Persist for one hour thinking only of ugliness. What do you notice? Record your findings. Compare your findings of ugly with beauty.

Let's get down to the business of how to change inwardly.

First: Become Conscious

This means observing your thoughts, feelings, words, attitudes, emotions, desires and the rest of your inner psychological workings. An excellent way of achieving greater self-awareness is by keeping a daily journal or diary. Record your personal ideas and feelings. Be as truthful and honest as possible. Avoid self-censorship. Call a spade a spade.

Second: Discover Your Genuine Interests

By getting acquainted with yourself through your journal or diary, you'll begin to see-feel-know what stimulates you. You may discover you love walking in the woods or down by the beach. Perhaps you enjoy music or conversation with certain friends. Whatever it is, you will know what genuinely interests you. Now, you must cultivate, nurture that interest, since it increases your zest and joy for living.

Third: Develop Constructive Thinking

Learn to form what you sincerely want to have, to do and become into concise words and clear images. Confused, indecisive words and pictures lead to disorganization and difficulty in daily life.

It may be necessary for you to buy or borrow books, which will aid you in developing your thinking ability. Three excellent books are: 1. How to Develop Your Thinking Ability by Kenneth S. Keyes, Jr., 2. Concentration: A Guide to Mental Mastery by Mouni Sadhu, 3. How to Think Straight by Robert H Thouless.

Fourth: Learn About Your Subconscious Mind

Whatever the conscious mind pictures or thinks with words is reflected into the subconscious mind. The subconscious has some kind of magnetic attracting force, which attracts what you have pictured, or put into words.

Repeated images and words influence you to the point of habit. Negative habits, maintained by the holding power of the subconscious, means you're locked into life patterns which seem impossible to change.

You can change through a step-by-step incremental process. Feeding the subconscious clear, positive, concise and accurate data means that gradually your outer life must change for the better.

Fifth: Cultivate Gratitude

Be thankful for what you do have, no matter how insignificant it may seem to you. Be grateful for your health, loved ones, job, food and so forth. Gratitude will tune you to the source of all change.

When disappointments arise, turn immediately to positive, grateful feelings. Once you've cultivated the healthy habit of gratitude, you'll see that your so-called disappointments were necessary stepping-stones to true, lasting and ongoing change.

Now that you know what to do, do it. Set up a plan of action. Channel your energies daily into:

1: Becoming Conscious
2: Discovering Your Genuine Interests
3: Developing Constructive Thinking
4: Learning About Your Subconscious Mind
5: Cultivating Gratitude

Before long you'll notice a difference in yourself. Others will see a change in you. Situations and events will be more compatible with your structure and function. Changing yourself from inside means continuous growth in all areas of your life.

Chapter 8
Rapports

What is a rapport? There are fundamentally two types of rapports: constructive and destructive. A constructive rapport is a harmonious synchronization of energies, vibrations, and frequencies. A destructive rapport is an inharmonious synchronization of energies, vibrations and frequencies.

Another way of explaining rapports is by way of the law of sympathetic vibration. When you meet a stranger or a new acquaintance have you ever felt you were on the same wavelength? Did things just seem to click between you? Then you were experiencing the effects of the law of sympathetic vibration, a rapport.

Perhaps you have similar backgrounds, similar experiences, similar philosophies, similar habits, etc. The frequencies in your personality patterns and psyches have nearly the same vibrational wavelengths. You are then in sympathetic vibration, in rapport with that person.

Depending on the quality of the vibrations, you can determine the quality of the rapport: constructive or destructive. If you find yourself on the jovial, calm, humorous, congenial side, then these are an indication that the rapport is constructive. On the other hand, if you feel off, irritable, negative, unnecessarily hostile, then more than likely you have established a destructive rapport.

To illustrate, an artistic, talented fellow was pursuing a singing career in New York City. In order to save money on rent, he found a roommate. His roommate had no interest whatsoever in the creative arts despite the fact that he was studying to be an architect.

No matter how hard he tried he could not land a singing job. He knew his voice was not at fault since he kept in constant vocal shape through singing lessons and daily practice. Gradually, he became almost imperceptibly disenchanted and then even resentful toward the people who witnessed his auditions. Unknowingly, this negative attitude made the situation even worse.

He began to feel slight pains in various parts of his body. He decided there must be something physically wrong with him, blaming his misfortune on some mysterious ailment. He saw doctor after doctor taking medical test after medical test but nothing physically could be found wrong with him.

Still, the pains persisted in the back, in the limbs, in the head and in the stomach. The doctor bills became so expensive that he could no longer afford his singing lessons. He became obsessed with his pains to the point where his interest in singing faded into the background.

When the doctors did not come up with the answer to his problems, he investigated alternative health methods. Acupuncture, vitamins, nutrition, fasts, water therapy, etc. became the quick cure all, the answer, but still the pains persisted. The struggling singer got to the point where he would try anything in order to overcome the pains, which, at times, were excruciating.

Somebody suggested a weekend yoga retreat in the country. The very first weekend retreat the pains disappeared completely. Saturday and Sunday were joyous time for him; he had found the answer. Now he could concentrate all his energy again on his singing career.

Monday morning the pains returned. The letdown brought on a deep depression. All week he sulked. He returned to the yoga retreat for a second weekend. The pains disappeared once again. He couldn't understand it.

Again, on Monday the pains returned. The young singer was desperate. He worked part-time in a famous Broadway restaurant. As chance would have it, he struck up a conversation with one of the customers who had some knowledge of rapports.

After telling his tragic story, the knowledgeable customer suggested he find another roommate. At first the struggling singer balked at the idea but being in such desperate straits he consented to give it a try. Within a week after his roommate moved out, the pains disappeared and within a month he landed his first professional singing job.

If you are not familiar with the effects of rapports then this story may sound amazing, really unbelievable. In fact, the story is a true one; a destructive rapport almost cost the young fellow his career. He was not aware of the roommate's negative emotional nature, destructive thought-feeling habits and envious attitudes.

The Buddha is claimed to have said in the Dhammapada, one of the Eastern religious text:

> If you do not have a friend
> Sober, pure and wise
> Walk alone – like a king who
> Has renounced a conquered
> Kingdom,
> Or an elephant roaming free
> In the forest.
> Better aloneness than the
> Friendship of a fool.
> Walk alone like an elephant
> Roaming free in the forest
> Be undemanding. Stay away
> From Unconsciousness.
> Choose friends virtuous and excellent
> Shun the low-minded and
> Ill-doing.

Begin to take careful note of the kinds of people you spend a lot of time with. There's an old saying that birds of feather flock together. In other words, those people you call friend will in some way, often in many ways, reflect your own tendencies, attitudes, habits, likes and dislikes, etc. Are you making constructive or destructive rapports?

What are some of the indicators of destructive rapports?

Physically: stomach pains, headaches, burning sensations in the back of the neck, heart stabbings, constipation, gas, sudden diarrhea, etc.
Emotionally: depression, feelings of loneliness, sadness, anger, self-pity, guilt, fear, etc.
Mentally: confusion, foggy-headedness, negative thoughts which have no basis in what's happening, thinking but you cannot remember what you were just thinking about, etc.

What steps can be taken to begin to break destructive rapports? Before steps can be taken, you first have to be aware of the two kinds of destructive rapports: a) short term and b) long term. Short-term rapports usually last from a few seconds to an hour or two, sometimes longer. One of the best ways to detach, non-identify with influences of a short-term destructive rapport is by slow attentive rhythmic breathing through the nose. Keep it up for five minutes or so. If the rapport persists, then continue for another five or ten minutes.

Short-term rapports can often be alleviated by getting out of a negative atmosphere or situation or by getting away from a negative person. Also, by bringing your focus, your attention away from identification with the rapport while it is happening will often help disconnect you from its influence.

Long-term destructive rapports are an entirely different matter. Often you are not even aware of them, much like the struggling young singer was not aware of his rapport. Usually it is some situation, person or place, which you have been exposed to for a long time so that the destructive influence almost seems normal.

Breaking a long-term destructive rapport, requires, first, considerable awareness and reevaluation of most all of the influences in your daily environment. Second, you must disconnect by putting less time, attention and energy into that situation, person or place. Sometimes you have been involved unknowingly with a destructive rapport for years so that it may take considerable patience for you to break, detach and non-identify with it.

In this chapter we have covered just a few of the basics as regards rapports. In reality, it is a deep, long and hard study of oneself in relation to the environment in order to unravel the intricate complexities behind rapports. Wise, conscious living necessitates some theoretical as well as practical knowledge of rapports.

Chapter 9
Your Spiritual Tuning

"Our generation is doing all its thinking in terms of power, energy, dynamics – the kind you read about, not in a book, but on a meter! Why not concede the reality of supernormal assistance, and encourage people to go after it?"

> Bobby Merrick (character)
> Magnificent Obsession (novel)

You must pay the price for Your Spiritual Tuning: "go after it" as Bobby Merrick says. Just because someone says they are "spiritual" or because they think they are "spiritual" or because they attend church, temple or mosque look like they are "spiritual" does not make them one wee bit "spiritual."

A true spiritual tuning comes only when contact is made with a conscious power. Bobby Merrick again:

"It would be just like all the rest of 'em ... nobody would want to go to all the bother and expense of making his own connections with his major personality ... he'd decide to sing about power! Watt didn't sing for his! And Faraday didn't produce the dynamo by reciting 'I believe in Volta, maker of the dry battery and father of the Leyden jar, and in his successor Ampere, who codified the formulae for electro-dynamics, and in Ben Franklin, who went at it with a kite ... No, sir! By the great horn spoon – not ... Faraday did his in an attic, alone, on an empty stomach!"

The quotes come from the enjoyable 1935 novel, Magnificent Obsession by Lloyd G. Douglas. The book was made into a movie with the same title in 1954. It starred Jane Wyman and Rock Hudson. The film version can be found on YouTube (2021) and from time to time on television.

In the movie version an aging doctor counsels Bobby Merrick with an enlightening analogy of why he is lost, restless and spiritually bankrupt. To paraphrase, it goes something like this:
"Do you see that lamp on the table over there?" (doctor)
"Sure." (Bobby Merrick)
"Well, you're like the lamp."
"How's that?"
"The lamp has a table to rest on; it has a base, it has the proper wiring and plug. It's a perfectly good lamp except ...
"Except for what?
"Don't you see? ... It's not turned on. It's not plugged into the power source. ... Therefore it's useless; it has no purpose. If the lamp was plugged in and turned on the bulb would light up and the whole room would be illuminated. It would no longer be useless; its purpose would be fulfilled."
"I'm not a lamp ...
"You're not plugged into the power source. That's why you feel useless, living without a purpose."

What prevents you from contacting the spiritual power, which would illumine your life with consciousness, knowledge, a zest for living and a rich life purpose? Before we can attempt answering this question, to some extent, let's take a look at the levels most of us live on day in and day out.

LEVEL 1: Physical Frequencies
Sensing
Tension
Dis-ease
Eating
Sleeping

Washing
Actions
Etc.

LEVEL 2: Psychological Frequencies
Memories
Images
Words
Thoughts
Feelings
Emotions
Desires,
Etc.

LEVEL 3: Spiritual Frequencies (After contacting the Conscious Power)
Perceptive Awareness
Conscious Use of Energy
A Conscious Co-Creator
A Craftsperson in Consciousness
Tuning to the Light Dimensions
Etc.

Most of us spend 99.999% of the time on the first two levels, physical and psychological. In fact, we are usually so identified with these two levels that we're like a radio believing foolishly that the sounds coming out of the speakers originates inside the radio.

The first step in contacting the conscious power, the true self, is to consciously detach, not identify so strongly and completely with the physical and psychological levels.

"So long as an individual is identified with his own psychological self [and physical self] or on a lower level believing that his thoughts originate in his cranium or brain (not knowing that his brain cells are like radio tubes, picking up waves and frequencies) can he know in that mind level substance the force or power we label the true self.

Vitvan, Christos Book 4

Getting back to our question: What prevents us from making conscious contact with a spiritual power?

FIRST – identification, almost totally, with the physical and psychological levels, believing your body is you, your thoughts are you, your feelings are you, your actions are you, etc.

SECOND – our ignorance and unconsciousness prevents us from contacting the power or our true self. And, what's worse, we are not even aware how ignorant and unconscious we really are.

THIRD – we have not paid the price; we have not gone after it. One of the main reasons for Gateway to Stardust is to show a way you can pay the price – earn Your Spiritual Tuning.

In order to make contact, to consciously connect with a higher intelligent power you must harness and refine the energies and forces of the psycho-physical organism. You must learn to live rhythmically. You must learn to handle your energies, your emotions, your relationships, your speech. You must know how to relax, digest past experiences and tap your creative energies. You must be more or less stable financially as well as having a keen, flexible awareness in every activity.

Harnessing your psycho-physical energies through mastering the Gateway to Stardust lessons will build the circuits or connections needed in order to consciously contact in a natural and scientific way the conscious power or true self.

"This thing I've been talking about is not in the field of ethics. It belongs rather to science. We have been at great pains to construct devices and machinery to be energized by steam and electricity and sunshine; but haven't realized how human personality can be made just as receptive to the power of our major personality.
Magnificent Obsession

Once you have harnessed, over a period of time, your psychological frequencies how can you become more spiritually tuned? As Plato said over two thousand years ago, you can contact the master self only through tuning in. What is the process of tuning in?

How does one "tune in" the major personality, true self, higher self, master self – whatever you want to call it? First and foremost there absolutely must be a deep sincerity within one's own consciousness. It is the sincerity and need which invokes, contacts the conscious power of the true self.

Agony, pain, suffering, crisis and conflict are the five culprits that prod us on, goad us into the possibility of growth, learning and ultimately contacting our deeper self. They provide the needed shocks, which heighten our awareness to what we are thinking-feeling-doing against the natural laws of right scientific living. The more conscious we and the more functionally we handle our agonies, pains, sufferings, crisis and conflicts the greater the possibility of connecting with a power and consciousness resonating at a higher frequency than our own.

By handling, structuring and channeling our psycho-physical energies creatively and constructively, we reduce the amount of noisy static in our mind-emotions-body. Then the transmission of the spiritual frequencies can be received without psychological interferences.

Using the functional tools given in Gateway to Stardust to order your daily life situations, you will build into your very body cells delicate receiving circuits, which will tune you into the natural order process patterns of the more conscious self. You will then gradually synchronize your frequencies with the frequencies of the more conscious self.

"When one breaks out of his own manifold of values, those of another or his race psyche, based upon and oriented to objective identifications, he becomes established on his own mind-level, his spiritual soul oversees the development of his psychic nature without interference."
Vitvan

It's difficult to give a specific functional exercise, which will tune you in to the spiritual frequencies. It proceeds differently from one person to the next, at different times, in different places and in different peoples. It unfolds differently and uniquely for everyone; and it's not usually an instant flash-shazam. It takes patient, steady, conscious effort through a process in time to make the connection strong, flexible and continuous.

However, by applying diligently the practical exercises outlined in Gateway to Stardust, you demonstrate both your deeper sincerity and your need to live your life more in tune with spiritual skills. Just how the process goes and what specific exercises or conditions assist you in making the initial contact, I cannot say. But it will scientifically and naturally happen as you grow in the natural order process.

What has been said in this chapter may sound like a whole lot of garble to some. All I can say is test it out. Use the scientific method: observation, experiment, experience and expression. If it works, use it. If not, discard it temporarily and say I.D., insufficient data.
"My body is wearing out, and when I can't tinker it back into service any more, I'll drive it out to the junk pile; but I don't have to be junked with it! I'm tied up to the major personality! ... like a beam of sunshine to the sun! ... If that's religion, Grandpere, I'm religious! But I'd rather think of it as science!"
Bobby Merrick, Magnificent Obsession

"Merrick – just a minute! ... We modernists have been trying to show how religion is not at odds with science. What we've got to do now is show how religion is a science! Isn't that what you mean?"
"Exactly! Nothing more or less than that! You have it! More power to you! See you in September!"
Magnificent Obsession

Chapter 10
The Prison and Poison of Fame and Fortune

"If I could walk around and see things without mobs of people, be free, it would be worth a million dollars, if only for a week! Just being little ol' me, instead of "the image", would be a relief after so many years."
Elvis Presley

A world-famous author recently wrote, "I hope to God I never have anything like the success of Elvis happen to me." This writer spent twenty years in the U.S. Coast Guard. During his stint, he taught himself to write.

He was an on-board cook. Then one day he began writing love letters for his fellow sailors. His letters were so successful that he was assigned full-time writing duties.

Eventually, he devoted some of his writing time trying to write for various newspapers and magazines. Eight grueling years later he made his first sale.

As time went on and his writing improved, he sold more and more. Finally, at 37, he retired from the Coast Guard in order to pursue writing as a career.

At first, he lived in Greenwich Village, New York City, in a one-room basement apartment. He says about those days, "I was literally hanging on by my fingernails, trying to make it as a magazine writer. I was selling just enough to make it from week to week, sometimes from day to day."

After writing his first book, he achieved some national recognition. He became an excellent interviewer, doing numerous interviews for Playboy magazine.

Have you guessed who? He was Alex Haley, the author of Roots, the biggest success in United States publishing history at that time.

The demands of his fame and fortune proved exhausting. The extensive travel to lectures and interviews drained him. He stopped writing for nearly two years. Finally, in desperation, he forced himself to slow down.

The fame and fortune had become a prison and a poison. His perennial dream of becoming a successful author turned into a nightmare. Finally, he decided to strive for a more moderate public image.

There are numerous psychological and semantic reasons why people crave fame and fortune. Power, recognition, insecurity, sublimation, greed and egotism are some of the psychological reasons. Identification, mistaking word for thing, not consciously abstracting are a few semantic reasons.

The newspapers, popular magazines, television and other media push and impress on the subconscious the glitter and glamour of fame and fortune. To be famous and/or wealthy is made to appear the pinnacle of happiness.

The misconception is: if you have fame and fortune, you can have whatever you want. Having whatever you want, means you'll never, ever have any cares or problems. Others will cater to your every need. Life, from then on, will be a breeze.

Any superficial investigation into the lives of the rich and famous pops the delusion bubble. Alex Haley had all the fame he wanted. He pushed it away, when it began to destroy him. Elvis Presley died a lonely man despite hundreds of millions of fans worshipping him. I could cite endless examples. I would suggest watching the documentary I Am produced and directed by Tom Shadyac as another example of the dead end of fame and fortune.

Let me clarify what I mean by fame and fortune. There is a

destructive and a constructive fame. There is the unbalanced, fanatical fame. And, there is a moderate, sane fame or recognition.

Most people are identified with the destructive sort of fame. This kind of fame is an addiction, and emotional-mental drug. This type of famous person must have his or her fix. Without his regular dose, he sinks into the pit of loneliness; no one cares.

Constructive "fame" should be more aptly called recognition. The recognition is for a talent, skill or work, which enhances the lives of those around him or her. Usually, this type of person is not obsessively seeking public recognition. If it comes with the skill, job or talent, then fine, but it is not at the top of the list of priorities.

There is competitive fortune and there is a creative fortune. The dog eat dog, survival of the fittest fortune is destructive. This type of person will stop at nothing to increase their personal money stash. They enjoy making the "big deal" through the use of gentleman's lying, fraud and deception.

Their motives are almost entirely self-centered. If individuals and groups hurt in the process, they usually justify it by chalking it up to "that's business." Their conscience has been silenced.

Those, on the other hand, who make their fortunes creatively are quite a different lot. Only a small percentage of the rich fall into this category. Nevertheless, the influence of these few is far-reaching.

The creatively rich always give more in use value than they receive in cash value. They encourage others by their actions, to improve their lot in life. They are rarely wholly materialistic. They take a moderate approach, developing themselves physically, mentally and spiritually.

The creatively rich do not want to enslave or hold back the poor and less fortunate. In fact, they want the poverty stricken to become as well off as they are. Indeed, they do not even like to view the poor as poverty stricken, but as individuals beginning the process of becoming creatively rich.

Jackie Thompson, author of The Very Rich, talks about the ten wealthiest in America. On February10, 1981, I ran a pendulum check on each. (See Beyond Pendulum Power, available on Amazon).

1: Mostly negative in the physical, energy, emotional and mental bodies.

2: Closed minded.

3: Drug taking, obsessed, emotionally exhausted, negative thinking.

4: Rigid thinking, emotionally disturbed.

5: Physically drained, immature, extremely unconscious.

6: Physically and emotionally negative.

7: Physically off, a lot of energy but chaotic, emotionally frustrated.

8: Ill, infantile, cunning, backstabber.

9: Fanatical, heart problems.

10: Sick, drugged, depressed.

Based on this one check, only 1 out of 10 of America's richest is creatively wealthy. The rest appear to be on the negative competitive side.

What can be done to avoid destructive fame and fortune? Become acutely aware of false fame and fortune. See it for yourself. Notice how it's pushed by the mass media. Be conscious of its effect on people. Learn to catch yourself when you think: "If only I had fame and fortune, I'd be happy." Let such thoughts go.

Your thoughts are impressed on the subconscious mind. The subconscious accepts your thoughts as is. It does not discriminate or filter out the negative thoughts.

Believing happiness comes just because of fame and fortune is a delusion. Alex Haley had his bubble burst. Why feed your subconscious a false belief?

However, if you persist in your false belief the subconscious will oblige you. You will attract circumstances and people that will contribute to your false fame and fortune.

Watch out! You just may get what you ask for. Then you will have to learn the hard way, if you learn at all.

To avoid living a lie of false fame and fortune, and to find true happiness, search out what it is you enjoy most. If you know already, continue and your subconscious will aid you every step of the way.

If you do not know what makes you shine from within with purpose, try the following. Before going to sleep at night ask with deep sincerity: please reveal to me, through dream, hunch, sign or event, what will make you happy, fulfilled person.

Repeat several times, until you feel the force of your request within. Know that you will receive a reply soon, maybe not the first day, but sometime soon. Once you find out what makes happy, learn all you can about it. Think about it. Do it.

Doing what makes you happy will lead you to cultivate other talents, skills, abilities, etc. Your success will bring you recognition from those you love and work with. Money for all your needs will be provided to you because of your inner fulfillment.

MIDNIGHT 2013

Presents fall like snowflakes
On frozen cornfields.
Souls fill like silos
At harvest time.
Light your fireplace heart.
Time melts at 32 degrees.
May happiness play
In your loving soul
From dawn till
Midnight 2013.

PART TWO

MYTHOLOGICAL THEMES IN ART, LITERATURE AND TATTOOS

Chapter 11
The Awakening in Art

Cyndee's The Awakening Series is comprised of eight oil paintings on 3' X 4' canvases. The paintings portray a transformative process within Cyndee's psyche, which resonates with the transformative process that goes on within us all. The Swiss psychologist, Carl Jung, called this process the "individuation process." In his book The Archetypes and the Collective Unconscious Jung defined the individuation process as the "transformation process that loosens the attachment to the unconscious." In other words, in order to grow and evolve as an individual we must use our human capacity to become aware of what is holding us back and then let go.

In the winter and spring of 2002 Cyndee painted The Awakening Series. At that time she was taking a Women Studies class at the University of Nevada, Reno. One of the novels on the reading list, The Awakening by Kate Chopin, focused on the struggles of a creative woman in a society that demanded a woman be a wife and mother, sacrificing any artistic purpose for her husband and children. The Awakening Series is named after Chopin's novel.

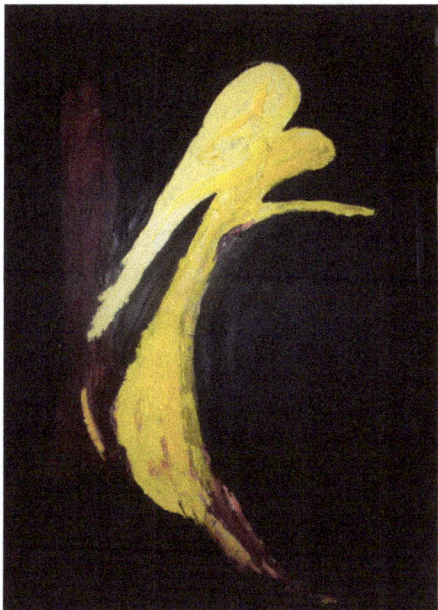

Painting One: Transformation

The background is black, the place of darkness, the cave, and the womb – the place of birth. A solar yellow angelic figure emerges out of a crimson red chrysalis. The chrysalis is the hard-shelled pupa from which a butterfly is born. This is an archetypal image of the transformation process, the worm-like larva transmuting into a winged butterfly.

In Cyndee's painting the crimson chrysalis symbolizes a crystallized pattern in her past that becomes a birthplace for a new, more conscious her. Red, crimson red is often associated with passion, blood and sacrifice. In women it has biological connections with the monthly menstrual cycle. For any woman who has given birth and for any man who has witnessed it, they can attest, giving birth is a bloody mess. Giving birth is a sacrifice, a letting go. It involves pain, often excruciating pain.

The solar yellow winged figure is born of the dried blood crimson. Notice one of the wings is free and the other is still caught in the chrysalis. The birthing process is not yet complete. In the lower crimson chrysalis there is still a sliver of solar light that has not yet attached itself to the right wing. This indicates a conscious effort is still required to complete the transformation.

In the heart area of the winged figure the crimson has magically appeared. In both eastern and western spiritual traditions the heart center accelerates in vibration when a certain awareness level emerges. The winged figure has not only broken out of the chrysalis, the heart center, it has awakened to a higher passion. There is a letting go of a lower vibration red for a higher vibration red – the individuation process has become a priority, a passion.

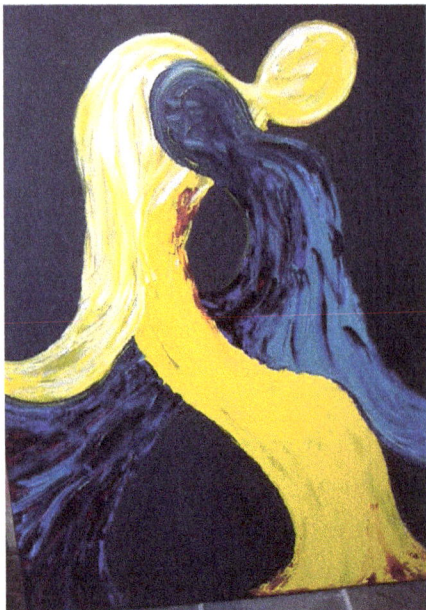

Painting Two:
Alchemical Marriage

In the Alchemical Marriage the black background still indicates the place of birth, the self-development process is going strong. The winged solar yellow figure is joined and intertwined with a dark blue figure. Dark blue is often associated with water and the feminine, yin energy. The male, yang solar yellow is intertwined with the female, water blue. The union of the opposites in alchemy was called the Alchemical Marriage. In Painting Two the thinking and feeling, male and female qualities are joining and show integration.

The two-winged figures have an undulating quality that is almost serpentine. In a way they are reminiscent of the physicians' caduceus entwined by two snakes. There's a combination of winged, spiritual energy, related to the air element and entwined snakes around an invisible staff. The serpentine energy is rising indicating an increase in awareness. Thought and feeling are not just focused on the mundane but on the inner workings of the soul.

Both figures have red in the heart center area. The Alchemical Marriage is a fiery union. Notice in the lower extremity areas there is also red. The legs and feet have to do with motion. This transformation has legs. Red is action. Not only is there thought and feeling, there is the power to put thoughts and feelings into action. Transformation is about acting based on new awareness.

Painting Three:
Four Elements

In Painting Three the solar yellow winged figure continues to be the central form. The blue figure has been replaced by three distinctly female figures. The blue watery feelings in Painting Two have heated up and morphed into three intertwined red womanly forms. The breasts suggest nurturing. The red shouts action.

A personal transformation has taken center stage both in thought and action. A woman's individuation process is more about nurturing than conquering.

For the first time bright white is emphasized in the color scheme. The white is around, on and near the breasts as well as on the wings. White, as any artist or physicist knows, is a combination of all seven-rainbow colors. White has strong associations with "purity" and "virginity." The pain, agony and bloody sacrifice in Painting One are about to be replaced by the peace and the repose that comes with a conscious connection with a spiritual power. The cave womb is a lighter black. Spiritual awareness has come to the place of birth.

Numerological symbolism stands out in Painting Three. There's the one solar male form and the three breasted red forms. The 3 and the 1 that is 4 pattern abounds in myth, dreams and fairytales. Jung wrote in The Archetypes and the Collective Unconscious, "Between the three and the four there exists the primary opposition of male and female, but whereas fourness is a symbol of wholeness, threeness is not." In other words the tension, the energy potential between male-female, positive-negative, threeness-fourness is generating an acceleration of life force being utilized in the individuation process. The same three/four pattern can be seen in the four elements. Fire, air and water are all in visible motion. The fourth element earth is not visibly in motion, appearing more inert. (The paintings are on 3' X 4' canvases.)

Painting Four: Womb Flight

Going from Painting Three to Painting Four a major integration of self occurs. Four in numerology is a feminine number. The solar yellow winged figure is pregnant with a kind of divine child, symbolizing a renewed self. Mother psyche is about to give birth to a blue and red child. The red fire and the blue water have mysteriously mixed. The child is not in the stomach/womb area. Rather, the heart center has become the womb, the place of rebirth. The Gnostic philosophers of ancient Greece described a process occurring in the heart as a spiritual rebirth. The child symbolizes that rebirth – individuation process/transformation. The solar yellow focal points shine within the emerging new self. The winged solar yellow figure breaking free in Painting One is now a pregnant mother.

The kinetic energy spins throughout Painting Four. The form is by no means static. The serpentine movements in Paintings Two and Three now undulates, swirl around and through the solar Madonna's body and wings. This mother is about to take flight. The black womb moves, breathes, expands and contracts. Birth is immanent.

Painting Five:
Spiral Fetus

The birthing process has taken center stage. A spiral fetus form takes up almost the entire canvas. All energy is focused on transformation. The clockwise rotation means the individuation process is a conscious one. The solar yellow, crimson red and virgin white carry on the color scheme of the previous paintings. The black background indicates the womb.

The solar yellow is concentrated in the head area indicating that awareness of the process has intensified. Still, white is the dominant color. White has to do with refinement, purity and integration. The sacrificial crimson red has softened in spots with the first appearance of pink, a combination of red and white. Pink has to do with unconditional love, giving without expectation of return.

Paining Five is less structured than the previous four paintings. The fetus is the rudimentary human structure. This would suggest the transformation is in the early formative phases. The concentration of life energy is profound. The mother artist is taking this painting very seriously. There's nothing whimsical or frivolous going on here. We have a window on the formation of life itself amplified ten-fold. A sonogram is not required. The bright and penetrating imagination of the painter propels the observer into the inner creative world where technology can never go.

the crimson red angels with white highlighted breasts. Now the three have become one, pointing toward a heightened sense of wholeness.

The female psychology clearly takes precedents in Painting Six. For a man self-transformation is about taking definitive action that changes behavior. He replaces a self-destructive way of doing something with a self-improved way of doing something. A woman focuses, feels, breathes and gives birth. Usually a lot of what happens is not well thought out. Rather, a woman lets nature take its course. She doesn't plan, over- analyze or direct. The self-transformation of the individuation process is deeply felt, sensed, intuited and allowed. There's a going with the flow. The outcome is more or less a surprise. Often a man attempts to figure out the outcome ahead of time. He thinks he knows what's going to happen. She doesn't know the outcome and doesn't pretend to know.

Painting Six: Birth Plosion

The male, solar yellow yang is gone. The crimson, pink, white and black remain. Painting Six is strictly the world of yin, female mother. The single spiral-fetus pattern in Painting Five has differentiated into numerous circular spiral-like forms. There appears to be a boundary between the pink and red. Yet, they are very much connected. Love pink and sacrificial red are sisters.

In the painting's southeast quadrant one can almost make out a red female form with breasts outlined in white. This form is reminiscent of the Four Elements painting that featured

Painting Seven: Rainbow Energy

The dynamic kinetic movement of Painting Four returns in Painting Seven. Seven is the number of transformation according to Pythagorean Mathematics and Astrology. There are seven colors in the spectrum. This painting has a range of colors including red, yellow, blue, white, pink, grey and black. All the colors used previously appear in this painting, The Awakening Series spectrum.

The previous six paintings have distinguishable forms – angel-like forms in Paintings One through Four, the spiral form in Painting Five and the figure-eight circular forms in Painting Six.

Painting Seven leaves the world of form and moves into a world of color energy. Form has boundaries. Energy is boundless. Trans-formation has to do with changing form. The formless energy is an intermediary state between an old form and a new one.

The pipping the shell or chrysalis theme from Painting One returns in Painting Seven. Old forms, patterns, beliefs and behaviors have been left behind. The individuation process is free to go in whatever direction required, desired and/or inspired. The serpentine brush strokes symbolize the sloughing off of the old skin. After a snake sheds its skin, it is most vulnerable to the elements. When a person attains a heightened awareness, their energy is more dynamic and the feelings more sensitive.

Painting Seven celebrates the inner process. It's a kind of Marti Gras painting. It's time to party, sing, dance and let your hair down. Celebrating the re-birth, the individual transformation and finding the pot of gold at the end of the rainbow, allows the artist to move past recognizable forms into a kinetic dimension.

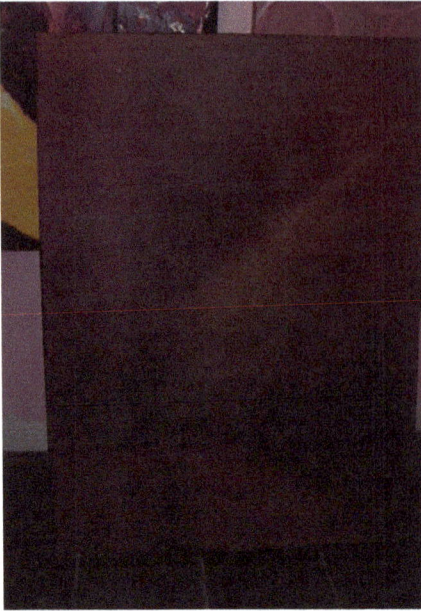

Painting Eight:
Black Hole Mass

In Painting Eight the previous seven paintings in The Awakening collapse into a black hole. Transformation spirals in endless cycles of birth, death and re-birth. The crimson and black merge creating a dried blood appearance. There's a faint white tint near the center of Black Hole Mass. No matter how dark, difficult, disappointing or depressing a psychological state, the white ray heralds the possibility of transformation, individuation and an awakening to another cycle of awareness.

Yellow swirls from the center toward the upper right. It is definitely not solar yellow. It is more like lunar yellow, reflected sunlight. The crimson black blocks its full power. A new transformational process begins. The dark yellow swirl may be the edge of another wing forming inside a chrysalis,

When Cyndee first showed The Awakening on July 2, 2002 at Reno's annual Artown, Painting Eight fell off the easel. No one saw what happened. Mysteriously, a tear in the upper left corner of the canvas shocked everyone. The artist was devastated. One of her children was damaged/ deformed. At the time, she couldn't stand having it on display. She removed it from the showing, a death. Death and transformation are forever hidden working their magic deep beneath the surface. Since then Cyndee has accepted Black Hole Mass back into the fold, although somewhat reluctantly.

Chapter 12
The Mythos in Harry Potter and the Philosopher's Stone

Chapter 1:
The Boy Who Lived

Chapter 1 begins with an end of the 20th century fantasy genre version of the universal divine child story that harks back to Moses, Horus, Jesus, Mithras, Krishna and a host of other divine child stories. Moses and Horus had their humble beginnings along the Nile River and Jesus in a Bethlehem manager. The divine child is placed in a basket, wrapped in swaddling clothes or in blankets like Harry Potter. The divine, symbolized by the light of spiritual consciousness, is confronted with the forces of darkness and the everyday unaware world of ignorance, fear and suffering. There are "other" worldly beings overlooking and protecting the child like the celebration by the three wise men after the birth of Jesus. The magical world beings assist the child. The first Harry Potter book introduces Albus Dubledore, Professor McGonagall and Hagrid from the world of the wizards and witches. We all have the divine spark, divine consciousness in potential within us. To actualize divine consciousness the hero must go on a journey going through various tests and trials. The struggle awakens the spiritual, divine consciousness.

Chapter 2:
The Vanishing Glass

Chapter 2 introduces the mythological, archetypal theme of the two brothers, two cousins. The dark = Dudley (fat, bully, blonde, spoiled) and the light = Harry (thin, black hair, magical, grateful). Ten years have passed. Harry must be about 11. Puberty signals the awakening of the kundalini serpent energies that can energize transmutations and transformations. The theme of the rejected stone = Harry, that will become the cornerstone emerges more clearly. He lives in a dark, dingy, spidery closet. He is not allowed to stay in the house alone. He is yelled at, mistreated and functions more as a slave than a loved nephew and cousin.

Other images that emerge in Chapter 2 are Harry's green eyes. Green is the color in the middle of the visible spectrum of light symbolizing equilibrium, peace and poise. Harry is not yet aware of his magical gifts. When something strange happens like his telepathic connection to the snake in the zoo everyone tries to rationalize or find a reason for what cannot rationally happen. When Harry spends long hours in his cupboard (closet) he sometimes has "strange visions" accompanied by green light and burning pain in his forehead. The awakening of inner vision, the third eye and 6th chakra energy center can be an ordeal. He rationalizes that the pain comes from the supposed car crash where his parents died.

Chapter 3:
Letters from No One

In Chapter 3 Harry, the hero embarking on the hero journey turns 11 years old. He is crossing the first threshold on his self-discovery journey. This is indicated by a break from the past and his ordinary life. The following are the events that mark Harry's major life change:

1: Harry is accepted and is going to Stonewall High School.
2: Harry moves his bedroom from the cupboard to Dudley's toy and playroom on the second floor.
3: Unexplained letters arrive for Harry day after day.
4: The Dursleys leave number 4 Privet Drive and end up on a rock island off the coast.
The letters are symbolic of Mer-

cury = Roman, Hermes = Greek and Thoth = Egyptian. This is the messenger god who represents Harry beginning a phase of learning and remembering the forgotten knowledge that will open the way to intuitive, psychological and spiritual levels.

Chapter 4:
The Keeper of the Keys

In Chapter 4 Harry begins to find out who he really is. Being under the influence of his aunt, uncle, and cousin has left him lacking in knowledge and steeped in ignorance. The sensory-based humans are unaware of other worlds, vibrations, and experiences. Additionally, they think it is crazy, weird and unreal. They are afraid of anything different or unusual and will discredit it as unrealistic. They want to be "perfectly normal". After all, they are Muggles, a person who lacks any sort of magical ability. They are unconscious and fear anyone who is conscious.

In the Ancient Greek mystery schools self-knowledge was the gateway to becoming conscious, self-fulfilled, and wise. Harry has been accepted into Hogwarts, a mystery school for wizards and witches. He is awak-

ening, becoming aware that he is not perfectly normal. By birthright he is a wizard.

Hagrid is the guardian at the threshold, who guides Harry to a more magical way of life. He has the keys to Hogwarts. He delivers the letters and opens the way for Harry to leave the unconscious, sense-based, humdrum world of the perfectly normal. In Chapter 4 Harry learns about Voldemort, the dark wizard, You-Know-Who. He is the fallen angel, a magician gone bad, a Lucifer. When one misuses **the force** for personal gain, they become like a dark wizard.

Chapter 5:
Diagon Alley

In Chapter 5 Harry has left the ordinary Muggle world of the perfectly normal and prepares to enter the magical world of Hogswarts. Hagrid assists Harry by shopping in London for uniforms, course books and other equipment. In order to shop Harry must access his inherited money from the underground Wizard's bank. A major mythological theme in this chapter is the gold in the dung, light is in the dark, and out of lead comes gold. In London Hagrid and Harry go to The Leaky

Cauldron, "a tiny grubby looking pub." It's a plane old place. No one would expect it mysteriously leads to Diagon Alley behind an old wall. There Harry purchases a cauldron, a snowy owl, and a custom fit magic wane.

The mythological story often has the hero discovering or acquiring the talisman with special powers in the most unexpected place. The "choosing" of the magic wand is described in some detail. The key here is the "wand chooses the wizard." The hero's wand, sword, lance, spear, etc. is not about materialism; it's about awareness, energy, and the vibrational compatibility between wand and wizard, spiritual power tool and hero.

To the hero, every person, place and thing has a vibration and a consciousness. To the Muggle materialists, people, places and things are objects that have no special quality. Note how Harry's cousin Dudley abuses his things by breaking and discarding them. Then he wants another object. He has no appreciation or gratitude.

Chapter 6:
The Journey from Platform Nine and Three-Quarters

Chapter 6 continues

to integrate the pagan and the modern. The pagan practices were prevalent throughout the Anglo-Saxon pre-Christian world, the ancient Roman Empire, ancient Greece and ancient and medieval Northern European and Mediterranean lands. The paganism is reflected in the emphasis on wizards, witches, wands, goblins, dragons, magic and spells. The Modern Era clearly comes through with the technologies like the computer, television, train, electricity, plumbing and the automobile.

Joseph Campbell, author of The Hero with a Thousands Faces, in his lectures and television appearances commented on how we are living in a time when meaningful mythological messages have been lacking. Mythological stories, he emphasizes, must guide, teach and speak to the inner and outer needs of the present world.

The Harry Potter story speaks to a 21st century digital generation by combining the ancient pagan with the modern. The "Chosen One" theme is further developed in Chapter 6. Everyone has heard of Harry Potter except Harry Potter.

He is shy, humble and naïve. His ego does not inflate

with fame. His chosen status can be compared to Dalai Lama who had notoriety as a baby and an infant child. Despite his Tibetan and world fame, he had gone through the most rigorous training just like the other monk trainees. Harry must train at Howarts just like the Dalai Lama trained for years in Lhasa, Tibet and then in exile in India.

Chapter 7:
The Sorting Hat

One of the Chapter 7 standouts are the four houses or dorms: Gryffindor (Harry's house), Hufflepuff, Ravenclaw and Slytherin. The esoteric traditions have variations on the use of four corresponding to the four life energies. This alludes to the four elements - earth, air, water and fire. Earth is reliable, stable and practical; air is mental, analytical, communication; water is feeling, emotional, empathetic; fire is action, movement and vitality.

The Swiss psychologist, Carl Jung, derived his four psychological types from the alchemists' four elements - thinking = air, water = feeling, sensation = earth and intuition = fire. The theme of four is universal and corresponds to the four cardinal directions, four colors, four universal forces, four seasons, four somatic divisions, etc.

The alchemists focused on the psychological mixing process involving the blending of the four elements to create the philosopher's stone, a symbol of integrated, wise consciousness. Jung labeled it the individuation process. By consciously integrating the four psychological functions a fragmented person could become whole. I would expect as book one unfolds the four houses would more clearly correspond with the four elements. Another mono-myth theme that stands out in Chapter 7 is the hero facing tests. Harry has crossed the threshold to Hogwarts - from the ordinary world to the extraordinary world. Harry's first test is the sorting ceremony. "Harry's heart gave a horrible jolt. A test? In front of the whole school?" By putting on the pointed wizard hat the Hogwarts house is determined. Harry imagines this relatively "easy" test to be far more difficult - no doubt a harbinger of more difficult tests to come. Chapter 7 also focuses on fear, the first enemy of a man or woman of knowledge according to the Yaqui Indians of Central America. Before putting on the sorting hat, Harry was nervous, anxious, and terrified.

Chapter 8:
The Potion Master

In Chapter 8 the motif of multiple levels of energy, states of consciousness and different dimensions continues. In Chapter 1 the Dursleys live along with other Muggles in the ordinary sensory world. Mr. Durlsey glimpses the world of the whispers, witches and wizards. However, he chalks it up to "it must have been a trick of light." In Chapter 8 the impermanence of "things" is emphasized. "Doors that weren't doors at all, but pretending." And "the coats of armor could walk." The magical world emerges into the ordinary world. Hogwarts has its resident ghosts like headless Nick and Peeves the poltergeist. Western and Eastern inner traditions emphasize impermanence. Heraclitus, a Greek philosopher, is famous for saying "No man ever steps in the same river twice." There is continuous change despite what the ordinary sensory world believes to be permanent. People, places and things are not solid and permanent as the senses lead us

to believe.

The Buddhist tradition is centered on change, impermanence and the doctrine of non-attachment. The Dalai Lama writes, "We must renounce our attachment to this temporal life; we must see that this existence is impermanent, whether it ends sooner or later." Professor McGonagall teaches transfiguration. She assigns her class to change a match into a needle. The only one with any success was Hermione. "It had gone all silver and pointy." A conscious person, a wizard, learns about change, transformation, and impermanence.

Chapter 9:
The Midnight Duel

Chapter 9 begins with the sentence, "Harry had never believed he would meet a boy he hated more than Dudley." The two-brother theme from Chapter 1 continues with the conflict between Harry and Draco Malfoy. It's not uncommon for the metaphor of conflict between good and evil, light and dark, consciousness and unconsciousness, etc. to be reflected in different places and faces. Again, according to the inner esoteric traditions the two-brother theme can be between male cousins, half-brothers or between schoolmates from different dormitories.

The brother story in mythology represents the struggle between the identification with the sensory and the spiritual consciousness that occurs within each person. Along as we are conflicted and stuck in identification with the opposites, the conflict within transfers from one place to the other, from number four Privet Drive to Hogwarts. Harry and Malfoy duel on their brooms at midnight. The Egyptian brothers Horus and Sut wrestle with each other at sunset. As the sun sets the light of Horus appears to be extinguished by the darkness of Sut. Still, in the morning the light gains victory over darkness. In Chapter 9 Harry, the light, prevails over Malfoy, the dark, at midnight, the witching hour. The darkness gives way to the beginning of the light of a new day at midnight. Often, in the dead of night, in our darkest hour, the dark night of the soul, we awaken to a greater light of consciousness. Harry out maneuvers Malfoy, the supposed master broom rider.

What is the significance of the broom and riding the broom? Traditionally, the witches (here the wizards) ride through the air on broomsticks. Air is the ancient element representing spirit - anima, pneuma, spiritus – the spiritual consciousness. In order to achieve an awakening to the awareness of NOW, the hero must overcome the forces of ignorance, over-coming the pull of gravity by flying. This requires making some sweeping changes. The broom removes the dirt, the mire of ignorance and unconsciousness. Dr. Alvin Boyd Kuhn writes in Hollowe'en: A Festival of Lost Meanings. "Knowledge is ultimately the only broom that will sweep out the psychological muck and dirt of the animal obsession." Toward the end of the chapter, Harry enters the forbidden corridor inhabited by monstrous three-headed dog.

In Greek mythology Cerberus, the three-headed dog guards the gate to the underworld. For the uninitiated, the underworld is off limits. Without the light of consciousness entering the underworld or the forbidden corridor is taboo. The three heads symbolize desire, fear and ignorance. Eventually, the hero must overcome these three limitations and emerge the victorious hero with the friendly dog of intuitive awareness.

Chapter 10: Halloween

The first part of Chapter 10 deals with Quiddich, the favorite Hogwarts sports pass time. Harry, after receiving his new state of the art broomstick, the Nimbus 2000, learns the Quiddich rules. The rules description is packed with number symbolism. There are seven players on each side. In esoteric philosophy the number seven occurs repeatedly. There are seven planets, seven days of the week, seven colors of the spectrum, seven alchemical metals, the seven psychological energy centers, etc. Each of seven has a positive and negative polarity, a yang for every yin. There are fourteen players in all, reflecting the cycle of the moon. It is a fourteen-day cycle from the New Moon to the Full Moon. There are three offensive (positive, yang) players called Chasers and three defensive (negative, yin) players, two Bludgers/Beaters and a Keeper. The seventh player is a Seeker, who represents the hero who conquers the conflict of the opposites – wins a game of Quiddich.

The second half of the chapter takes place on Halloween, October 31. According to Dr. Alvin Boyd Kuhn, the "Holy Night" or "Hallowed Even" is forty days after the autumn equinox on September 21. Forty days symbolizes "the interval of death of the germ of new life when incubated in matter. It was the symbol of the dark interval proceeding the dawn of a new cycle." Traditionally, Halloween allows for the temporary unleashing of the elemental animal energies. Harry takes on the primordial element of earth represented by the giant troll. He wants to rescue Hermione, symbolic of the soul. By becoming aware and living in the NOW we all have the possibility of slaying the dragon, the troll of unconsciousness, ignorance and unruly desire. Harry defeats the troll, at least temporarily, by sticking his wand up its nose.

What can this possibly mean symbolically. One interpretation is when the positive power = wand enters the troll's nostril = the negative power there is an awakening or acceleration of consciousness by balancing the opposites, "even a troll will notice." It ought to be noted that the confrontation with the troll takes place in the girls' bathroom, the place of elimination. This symbolizes the need to eliminate unconsciousness in order to experience heightened awareness. The troll has a disgusting smell. "Harry sniffed and a foul stench reached his nostrils, a mixture of old socks and the kind of public toilet no one seems to clean." In a sense by noticing the foul stench of unconsciousness, one can transform the negative into the positive greater awareness.

Chapter 11: Quidditch

In Chapter 11 November turns cold. The sun shines less and less each day. The powers of light, consciousness and the metaphor of wise action tend to diminish during the late fall and winter seasons. The hero symbolically is submitted to the trials of the dark night of the soul. Hogwarts is located in the mountains. Traditionally, the mountains are the symbol of the spiritual height, the spiritual frequencies. Hogwarts is next to a lake. In Egyptian esoteric philosophy there were two pools, the pool of the north and the pool of the south. Hogwarts is in the north next to a northern lake.

In most spiritual tradi-tions the north is the direction assigned to spiritual awakening. Saint (Santa) Claus lives at the North Pole. The cold drives people indoors in order to keep warm. The "outer" everyday world is "south", the world of negativity, unconsciousness and unruly passions.

Harry is "really lucky to have Hermione as a friend." She's the yin to his yang, the receptive (feminine) to his active (masculine). Hermione guides Harry through his homework. Beatrice guides Dante through paradise. By paying attention to the energy, vibration and feelings of the psyche, the soul, the hero can find his or her way through the struggles and challenges of the "cold", harsh world of nega-tive, destructive influences.

The antagonism between Snape and Harry continues. There's no love lost here. Snape is familiar with and teaches protection from the Dark Arts. The Dark Arts are a metaphor for negative thoughts, feelings, and actions. When we identify with negative energies and act on them a pulse recurrent frequency is set up, a habit pattern that lim-its our conscious participation in purpose, poise and mindfulness. The three-headed dog guarding the secret something – potion, treasure, magic talisman, sword, etc., has bitten Snape. His leg is "bloody and mangled." We are bitten by negative energies and lack of unawareness when we do not follow the path with a heart. We are wounded and, therefore, not capable of functioning at our best.

The dog bite occurs on Halloween when symbolically the animal instincts reign. Snape apparently uses dark magic on Harry during the Quidditch match "He had his eyes fixed on Harry and was muttering nonstop under his breath." Hermione comes to the rescue. "She crouched down, pulled out her wand, and whispered a few well-chosen words." When we listen to our intuitive thoughts and feelings, we can counteract the forces of darkness, those negative identifications that drain us of life force. Along those same lines, while Snape is cursing Harry "his broom was vibrating so hard, it was almost impossible for him to hang on much longer." After Hermione steps in "Harry was suddenly able to clamor back on to his broom."

Chapter 12: The Mirror of Erised

Harry gets to stay at Hogwarts for Christmas. Most students go home except for Harry and few other students. "He didn't feel sorry for himself at all; this would probably be the best Christmas he'd ever had." Christmas means Christ-birth. The mas is from the Egyptian mes "to be born" Mess-iah means the "(new) born Iah" (Jah), Jehovah, - God.

The common room and Great Hall "had roaring fires." The wooden logs created by nature speak of the everyday person under the influence of the topsy-turvy life. The roaring fires represent the spiritual flame of awareness transmuting ignorance into knowledge and unconsciousness into perceptive awareness.

There are twelve towering Christmas trees in the Great Hall. The twelve trees reference the twelve higher frequency energies latent within each human being. Spectacular decorations adorn the hall. Holly and mistletoe "hung all around the walls." Mistletoe grows in the upper branches of an oak tree deriving sustenance from its host. Similarly, the higher consciousness awakens from the natural day to day struggles of life. Each holiday season lovers kiss under the mistletoe sprig symbolizing "the union of the human and the divine, or male and female (yin-yang), elements, the "kissing" or commingling of which bring the Christ to his birth" (Kuhn). The holly sprig repeats the awakening, birthing theme of divine energies and consciousness. The red holly branch symbolizes the fiery spirit; the fruit and flower of a life lived consciously.

On Christmas morning Harry awakes to "a small pile of packages." Growing up with the Dursleys, he never received Christmas presents. This year he received six. Hagrid gave him a whittled wooden flute that sounded like an owl. The air element and the owl symbolize the vibration that overcomes the gravity of earthly materialism and sensory unconsciousness. The gift, however, that stands out the most is the invisibility cloak which when worn makes Harry's body invisible. As the initiate grows through the degrees of initiation he or she learns to become invisible. This means keeping your big mouth shut (KYBMS) and minding your own business (MYOB). From an energy-being perspective it func-

tionally means going into neutral and registering but not reacting.

Chapter 12 gets its name from the mirror of Erised. As Dumbledore explains, "It shows nothing more or less than the deepest most desperate desire of our hearts. It will give us neither knowledge or truth." The keywords are "desperate desire." Strong desires are attachments to memories, thoughts, feelings, experiences, and emotions that are powerfully charged either positive or negative. When we reflect, becoming inwardly conscious, of the past, we become aware of where we are subconsciously fixated to traumas that block us from knowledge and truth.

Chapter 13:
Nicolas Flamel

In Chapter 13 Dumbledore admonishes Harry, "the mirror could drive you mad." Previously in Chapter 12 the mirror is described as "high as the ceiling with an ornate gold frame, standing on two clawed feet." The clawed feet denote the instinctual, lower brain vibration. When we are under the influence of the compulsive instincts we are unsane. If we identify with unconscious, automatic drives, energies, and forces, the past rules. We prevent ourselves from living in the present, experiencing the clarity, wisdom, joy and bliss of the NOW. Dumbledore as the embodiment of the wise old man archetype counsels Harry on avoiding identification with what American master Vitvan labeled "images in the mind made substantive."

In Chapter 13 Harry finds out the identity of Nicolas Flamel, the "only known maker of the sorcerer's stone." It's unfortunate the American publisher, Scholastic, corrupted the author's original words philosopher's stone to sorcerer's stone. Apparently, the reasoning goes that American readers would associate the word philosopher with the word philosophy, associating it with hard to read and understand. The tradition of the philosopher's stone goes back thousands of years and is often associated with the alchemical tradition. Additionally, the word philosopher means lover of wisdom from the Greek words philo, love, and Sophia, wisdom.

According to the Swiss psychologist, Carl Jung, the philosopher's stone is an archetypal image of wholeness. In alchemy, the philosopher's stone is a metaphor for the transmutation of base metal in gold. Jung referred to this transformation as the individuation process. When we fully embrace our path and consciously choose to be mindful, we awaken to the process of raising our base metal unconsciousness into the gold of awareness in the present moment. Jung wrote in his book Man and His Symbols, "Medieval alchemists, who searched for the secret of mater in a pre-scientific way, hoping to find God in it, or at least the working of divine activity, believed that this secret was embodied in their famous 'philosopher's stone.'

Harry reads from the "enormous old book" that Hermione pushed toward him, "the ancient study of alchemy is concerned with making the philosopher's stone, a legendary substance with astonishing powers. The Stone will transform any metal into pure gold." Also, according to this same tome, Mr. Nicolas Flamel, an old alchemist, is the owner of the "only Stone currently in existence." The philosopher's stone "produces the Elixir of Life, which will make the drinker immortal." As we eventually become integrated, whole, and fully aware in the NOW we drink the Elixir of Life.

This is a metaphor for the spiritual frequencies of light. The ego-bound person, symbolized by Snape, projects immortality on the false personality or ego. Fluffy, the three-headed dog, guards the philosopher's stone. We cannot experience the sweet vibrations of the elixir until we let go our attachments to selfish thoughts, feelings and desires.

Chapter 14: Norbert the Norwegian Ridgeback

Chapter 14 focuses primarily on the "monsters" Norbert the dragon and Fluffy the three-headed dog that guards the philosopher's stone. Joseph Campbell in the PBS series The Power of Myth talks about the two dragons. The traditional European dragon "guards heaps of gold" and "psychologically symbolizes the binding of oneself to one's ego." In contradistinction, the Asian mythic dragon is a representation of the awakened dragon, kundalini energy that has transformed in spiraling stages through becoming more conscious. Norbert seems to be a blend of both, having negative and positive characteristics. Hagrid apparently wins the black dragon egg at a gambling and

drinking joint. This is followed by hot incubation of the black egg in Hagrid's hut leading to the birth of the elementary, unruly infant dragon. Potentially, the enlightened power, mindfulness and wisdom will emerge. Since dragons are against the law, Harry, Ron, Hermione and Hagrid want to hide yet protect Norbert. In order to lift up the serpent dragon energy there must be a steady, unrelenting and rhythmic effort to be conscious, wise, knowing, understanding and energy functional. The ancient Greeks used the word drakon meaning the keen-eyed seer. Apollo the seer, solar god overthrows the "lower" instinctive fiery dragon energy. The Babylonians had the hero Bel, the Christians had the archangel Michael (associated with the fire element) and the Hindus had the Naga dragon.

The fact that Hagrid uses books (knowledge) to parent Norbert represents the importance of knowing (Gnosis for the Greeks). Hagrid learns to feed the baby dragon on brandy and chicken blood. Brandy is distilled wine with a high alcohol content. Hagrid mixes it alchemically with chicken blood creating a reddish concoction. To transform our unconscious, automatic, culturally conditioned dutifulness we must consciously let go, non-identify and sacrifice, allowing for the acceleration of vibration by becoming more and more aware.

Hagrid learned from a dragon book that the growing baby dragon requires feedings every half hour or 48 times a day. Forty-eight is 4 x12. One interpretation is the awakening of consciousness on the four somatic levels: generative center, solar plexus center, heart center and the crown of the head center. As Norbert grows out of early infancy he eats dead rats washed down with brandy. Norbert's digestive system can extract nutrients from dead, uncooked rat meat. As we evolve, we can transmute the disgusting, the putrid, and the rotten into the alchemical golden awareness.

The other "monster" in Chapter 14 is Fluffy, the three-headed dog guarding the philosopher's stone. The line "Dumbledore knows how to get passed Fluffy" indicates that Dumbledore symbolizes the awakening, wise, compassionate self that masters the debilitative forces of fear, greed and desire, the three-headed dog. Backing up Fluffy and protecting the philos-opher's stone are six enchantments or spells wielded by six Hogwarts magical arts professors.

Chapter 15: The Forbidden Forest

In a 2008 interview J. K. Rowling said, "everything I have written, was thought of for that precise moment when Harry goes into the forest ... it is the last truth of the story" (El Pais Interview). Hogwarts students are warned from the start not go into the forest. From the beginning Harry breaks the Hogwarts' rules. He goes into the forbidden forest for the first time in Chapter 13 when he spots "Snape entering the forest on the run."

The forest is a place of darkness, danger, and destruction. The hero leaves the ordinary world in order to have an adventure, to awaken and expand consciousness by confronting fear, shadowy forces, and unconscious personality traits. Jung refers to the forest as emblematic of the "unconscious". Francois Nesbitte, a student of Joseph Campbell, emphasized that the unconscious is really not unconscious. It's fully alive, vibrant and energetically conscious. We are unconscious of it. By going into the forbidden forest Harry, symbolic of the hero/heroine in us, begins the process of discovering what forces lurk and prowl in our unknown shadow world.

Harry enters the forbidden forest at 11 pm. It's the 11th hour. Time is approaching the dark hour of midnight. Hagrid guides him. The forest is dangerous enough in the light of day but at night it is even more foreboding. Harry meets up with three otherworldly mythological figures, the centaur, the unicorn and cloaked figure that drink the silver blood of the unicorn.

The centaur is half human and half horse. As we begin to walk the path with a heart and learn about cosmic laws – the structure, function, order of cosmos – we awaken to our deeper humanity. Interestingly, the centaurs Harry meets follow the stars, symbolic of a higher order of law that acknowledges the inner path of self-awareness, inner purpose and individuation. When we rigidly adhere to society's rules, we repress, retard, and reject the blessed voyage of consciousness leading into the unknown world, the forbidden forest. The unicorn with silver blood (silver relates to the lunar,

female energies) symbolizes the purity of spirit that emerges by following our heartfelt path toward greater mindfulness, wisdom and compassion. The hooded figure that crawls "across the ground like some stalking beast" is none other than our false personality, our limited ego consciousness.

When we choose a spiritual path, the energy we experience is an exhilarating elixir that can inflate ego consciousness. An inflated ego attributes the energy "high" to itself. A false feeling of power blinds one to the greater reality, a knowing that we are integrated in a cosmic process where ego consciousness is a minor player and not the be all an end all. Firenze the centaur says to Harry, "it's a monstrous thing to slay a unicorn. Only one who has nothing to lose, and everything to gain, would commit such a crime. The blood of a unicorn will keep one alive, even if you are an inch from death, but at a terrible price."

The Yaqui Indians call this behavior the second enemy of a man of knowledge, power. Facing our fears and discharging their blinding identification leads to clarity of mind, heightened awareness – the third enemy of a man or woman of knowledge. At that point we are tempted by a personal selfish power so seductive it often goes unnoticed. If we succumb, we drink the silver blood of the unicorn, destroying an opportunity for divinity that embraces service, sacrifice and compassion.

Chapter 16: Through the Trapdoor

Neville admonishes Harry, "I don't think you should be breaking any more rules!" The hero or heroine is the rule breaker. He or she does not follow the tried and true path of societal duties, traditions and conventions. The hero takes the inner individual path yet at the same time respecting the rules laid out by current culture, in this case Hogwarts.

In order to take and stay on the path with a heart, the hero must silence the blind, mechanical adherence to unconscious thought, feelings, emotions and actions.

Ron, Hermione and Harry symbolize the triune conscious forces required to take and stay on the path to heroic achievement. Although Harry, Ron and Hermione exhibit multiple behaviors of great action, metal

acumen and timely sacrifice, generally Harry represents action, Ron sacrifice and Hermione logic. Neville symbolizes the rule follower, the tendency in each of us that plays it safe, doesn't rock the boat, and does the "right" thing. Hermione had to give Neville the full body-bind. In other words, we need to know when and how to eliminate or silence, the tendency to political correctness.

Next, Harry silences the three-headed dog with the magic musical flute. "From the first note the beast's eyes began to droop ... the dog's growls ceased – it tottered on its paws and fell to its knees, then it slumped to the ground, fast asleep." The flute is a wind instrument. Air symbolizes the spiritual frequencies. Music brings order and harmony to the bestial, animalistic energies of uncontrolled desires, unbridled ignorance and rampant selfishness.

In order to reach the philosopher's stone, symbolizing the integration, individuation and wholeness of an evolved human being, Harry must pass through seven doorways. Using correlative thinking, the seven doorways are the seven planets, the seven colors, the seven metals and the seven energy centers. As we master our energies, become an energy being rather than an unconscious sensory being, we move through levels of initiation, through doorways leading to a whole, spiritual being receiving the boon of the philosopher's stone.

After Harry, Hermione and Ron drop through the trapdoor, they make a soft landing on a "plant thing." The plant wrapped snakelike tendrils around them preventing them from moving to the next door. Hermione freed herself. The more Harry and Ron "strained against it, the tighter and faster the plant wound around them."

A conscious person learns that whatever you fight against becomes stronger. A basic law of human energy is energy follows attention. Whatever we focus on we give and feed energy. If we struggle, fight, resist excessively, we feed energy to that which we do not want. In a sense we become our own worst enemy. The hero in each of us must learn to non-identify, let go and go into neutral. By the end of Chapter 16 Harry passes through all seven doorways and enters the last chamber where the philosopher's stone lies unprotected from mis-

guided selfish energies symbolized by Snape and/or Voldemort.

Chapter 17:
The Man with Two Faces

The final chapter of Harry Potter and the Philosopher's Stone boils over with mythological symbolism. Harry expects Snape or Voldemort in the last chamber. Both are archetypes of the dark aspects, the light that has been obscured by selfish tendencies. Instead, Harry is surprised to see Professor Quirrell who he believed to be a "good" guy. False innocence can be the darkest of the dark. Evil masquerades as good. The deception runs deep. When we deceive ourselves into believing how "good" we are we are behaving like Quirrell. Harry soon discovers that Quirrell is the man with the two faces. When a person is "two faced," they are a fraud and a liar. We often lie to ourselves believing we are "honest" and "truthful."

Ultimately, it turns out that Voldemort, the personification of our dark, unconscious shadow self is present. He possesses the mind-head of Quirrell. "Where there should have been a back to Quirrell's head, there was a face, the most terrible face Harry had ever seen. It was chalk white with glaring red eyes and slits for nostrils, like a snake." The remnants of the reptilian brain live on in each of us located in the back of our heads. Voldemort demands, "Now give me the stone, unless you want to have died in vain." The lower reptilian brain wants the stone for selfish reasons falsely believing it will give unlimited ego powers.

Harry responds, "NEVER!" When we choose to be aware, we say NEVER! to selfishness and unconsciousness. Voldemort commands Quirrell to kill Harry but is unable to keep his hands-on Harry's neck. Physical contact with Harry's skin burns Quirrell's palms. Later Dumbledore essentially tells Harry that dark energies are transmuted by love. In other words, a higher frequency consumes a lower frequency, a transmuting action. "If there is one thing Voldemort cannot understand, it is love. Quirrell, full of hatred, greed, and ambition, sharing his soul with Voldemort, could not touch you for this reason. It was agony to touch a person marked by something so good." Harry survives the ordeal, the life or

death crisis and is reborn on a new level of consciousness. He has passed his first-year final exams, outwardly and inwardly.

Now the hero receives the reward. It appears that Slytherin will win the house cup for the seventh year in a row. However, after Dumbledore awards additional house points to Gryffindor, they win the house cup. "The huge Slytherin serpent (lower selfish brain) vanishes and a towering Gryffindor lion took its place." The lion is associated with the height of solar power in the summer, Leo the astrological lion. Light overcomes darkness. Thus, Harry completes the hero journey cycle by returning to the ordinary world of number 4, Privet Drive and the Muggle lives of uncle Vernon, aunt Petunia and cousin Dudley. The question remains – does Harry return with the elixir? In other words, will his new knowledge, experience and wizard consciousness change the Muggle lives of his ordinary family?

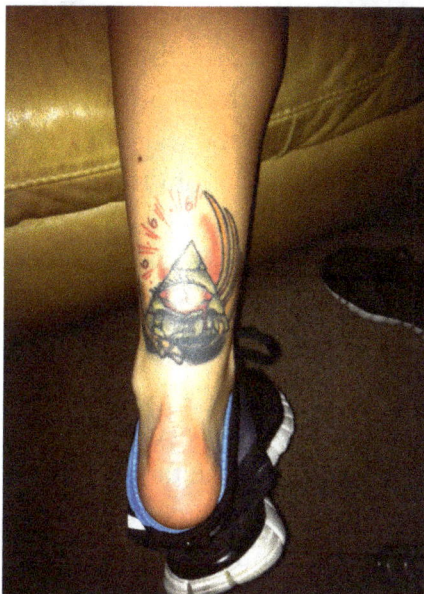

Chapter 13
Tattoos & Mythological Imagery

The Eye of Horus

The eye of horus tattoo is located on the back of the left ankle. To the ancient esoteric traditions, the body areas were significant. The ankle is related to the astrological sign Aquarius and the planet Uranus. The meaning resonates with innovation, change, creativity and knowledge. The fact that it's on the left side associates it with the feminine, yin, receptive and subconscious vibrations of the human experience.

Additionally, the English word ankle derives from the Egyptian word Ankh, meaning love, life and tie. Love's binding force joins the positive polarity, yang and the negative polarity, yin. Furthermore, the ankle is located in what the ancient Egyptians called the "south half." To the Egyptians, the "north half" is located from the waist up and the "south half" from the waist down.

The symbolism refers to the titanic struggle between the forces of automatic, habit energies (south half) and the conscious, aware, Now energies (north half). The imagery of the tattoo represents the bringing of awareness to daily life and acknowledging that the habits of the past are no longer going to rule. Instead, awareness will shine light on the dark places of the soul.

The divine eye is central to the tattoo and placed in the center of the triangle. Again ancient Egyptian symbolism shines light on the meaning. The Eye of Horus, as it was referred to in Egypt, represents the awakening to "spiritual" awareness. Spiritual awareness results from the functional, day-to-day efforts to be aware by focusing on the Now. It's a state of wordless awareness, bare attention and mindfulness.

The equilateral triangle symbolizes the balancing of the three life energies – positive, negative and neutral, or the balancing energy. When we are too negative, we cast ourselves into the dark night of the soul. When we are too positive, we experience flights from the present moment usually leading to an inevitable crash into suffering.

It's significant that an upside-down Christian cross is in the center of the eye. In Christian mythology, St. Peter was crucified upside down because he felt he was not worthy of being crucified upright like Christ. Incarnating in a physical body is an inversion of the light of spiritual consciousness. The lower frequencies of life in the flesh can be symbolized by the inverted cross.

In order to resonate with the higher frequencies (the Christ upright cross), one needs to acknowledge ego pride and deluded feelings of superiority. The blood tears flowing out of the lower portion of the eye symbolize this. Aligning with spiritual frequencies requires that one let go, sacrifice, non-identify with the physical body and egocentric, sense-based living.

The confluence of symbols including the upside down cross, the blood tear sacrifice and the divine eye of awareness are tattooed in the south half ankle area. Still, the three red sixes, 666, further underscore them.

There's a lot of misinformation and misinterpretation around the number of the beast. The Greek language scholar, James Pyrse, wrote an esoteric interpretation of the Book of Revelations titled the Apokolypse Unsealed, copyright 1910.

The English translation reads, "Here is cleverness (Sophia in Greek). He who has the Nous, let him count the number of the beast; for it is the number of a man and his number is 666." Pyrse explains, "As numbers are expressed in Greek by letters of the alphabet, and not by arithmetic figures, the number of a name is simply the sum of the numerical values of the letters composing it. Thus the numerical value of He Phren (the Greek word for lower mind) is 666."

When one incarnates in this dense frequency world, the influence of the Nous or higher mind are reduced and even eclipsed. The fact that the 666 are tattooed in blood red indicates the sacrifice of lower-mindedness. It's interesting to note that when 666 are added up it totals 18. Ancient Greek numerology adds up the 1 + 8 equaling 9, the Greek number for the Intuitively Wise.

Dr. Brittni Grider – The Eye of Horus Tattoo

Brittni wanted an Illuminati tattoo. To her this meant an image that resonated with her "free thinking" belief that required a conscious rebellion against the dark aspects of the European Enlightenment. The arrogant "American privilege" was built on the blood sacrifice of non-Europeans that included African slaves, indigenous American tribes and those with an Aztec heritage. The open eye inside the pyramid expresses a willingness to see these truths.

Minaret Temple Tattoo

The minaret temple tattoo is located on the upper inside of the left arm between the elbow and the bicep. The left side is often associated with the feminine goddess energy. Since the tattoo is not immediately visible to others, there's a mysterious quality. The arm symbolizes strength. Being on the left side, it refers to intuitive, spiritual strength and resilience.

The tattoo's central image is of a minaret temple, rising upward toward domes at the top. The minaret is a feature of Islamic architecture. However, it's not strictly Islamic since its origins are in Babylonian ziggurats, Egyptians pyramids and Chinese Buddhist pagodas. This inspired architectural form celebrates a higher power, frequency and energy. In Islam the minaret is the place where the call to prayer is sent out. Temples, mosques, cathedrals and synagogues are built to be a connection with vibrations that spiritually empower and nurture the psychological self.

In Arabic minaret means the place of fire or light. The English word fire has origins in the words pyre and pyramid, also places of fire and light.

Kuhn writes in his book The Lost Light, "The soul must be tied down in its linkage with the deeply hidden energies of matter and body until the fiery potencies at that level refine and purify its grosser elements."

The minaret temple tattoo is a highly detailed visual creation incorporating numerological symbolism. There are three minarets towers on the top level of the temple, one larger central tower and two small adjacent towers. Surrounding the three central towers are four smaller minarets.

Here we have the number symbolism of the three and the four that can be found universally in science, mythology and religion. Science acknowledges three atomic forces: positive proton, negative electron and neutral neutron. Mythological and religious iconographies resonate with a threefold differentiation of the one power to be conscious. The Hindus celebrate Brahma the creator, Shiva the destroyer and Vishnu the preserver energy. In the Egyptian mythos there is Ra the masculine solar energy, Isis the feminine receptive energy and Horus their offspring resulting from the union between Sun and Earth, Light and Life, Positive and Negative polarity.

The four smaller minaret towers symbolize the four directions, four seasons and four elements. Earth, water, fire and air are a quaternary corresponding to the four somatic divisions. Earth vibrates to the base of the spine area, Water to the solar plexus area, Fire to the heart area and Air to the head region.

The minaret tower has four levels three upper and a fourth lower level at the bottom comprised of a spiral staircase. In order to reach the spiritual heights (frequencies) of the three upper levels you must make a conscious effort to climb the stairs upward step by step. The spiral pattern is found throughout the natural universe from galaxies, to plants, to nautilus and starfish, to spiral patterns inside and outside the physiological organism (the body). For example, the spiral is found in the ear and the ratios in the body geometry.

It's interesting to observe that at the bottom of the spiral staircase is a plant like curl with a green leafy plant below that. Self-development emerges naturally from an organic process nurtured by the light of awareness.

Color symbolism contributes to the underlying significance of the minaret tower. There are essentially three colors used, blue-green, golden-orange and purple (a combination of red and blue). The spiral staircase below has the blue-green hand railing with the golden-orange stairs. Blue symbolizes the water and emotion and green symbolizes growth. Orange occurs from the blend of red and yellow. The golden-orange steps indicate that progress is made by intellect (yellow) combined with action (red). The golden hue in the stairs indicates the light of awareness required each step up the winding staircase.

Above the spiral staircase the purple color dominates. Purple is at the higher frequency end of the color spectrum. Purple combines red (action) with blue (feeling). When actions are guided by intuitive feelings the spiritual frequencies are experienced. Spiritual experiences are the mythological theme represented and experienced by archeological structures rising toward the heaven of functional consciousness.

Gabrielle Marangi Minaret Temple Tattoo

Gabrielle's original idea was an image that invoked the feeling of a "queen and her castle." Before meeting with the tattoo artist, she found an image of a mosque with four spiraling minarets surrounding it. This image provided a starting point for the artist. At the appointment the two then collaborated on refining the idea. As they discussed the tattoo, a song played. It was the Gothic rock classic "Temple of Love" by the English band Sisters of Mercy. The castle made by the artist then evolved into the Minaret Temple Tattoo.

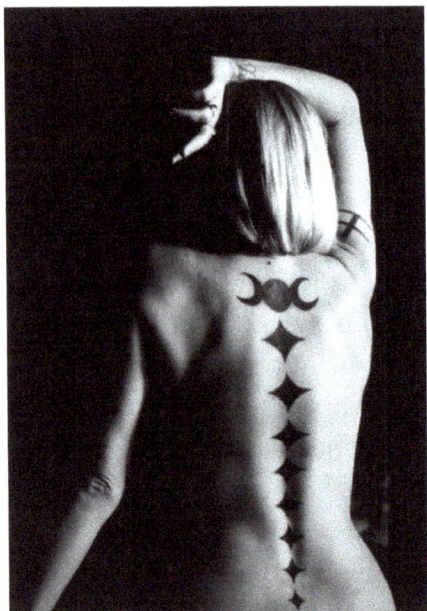

Lunar Diamond Tattoo

The central images of the lunar diamond tattoo are the nine black diamonds, the two crescent moons and the new moon. Tattooed along the spinal column, the nine diamonds rise from the base to the heart level. They are feminine, yin diamonds since the four sides are curved rather than straight. Moreover, the diamonds increase in size

from smaller at the base to largest at the heart level.

When one evolves by becoming more conscious, especially inwardly through self-remembering, self-observing and self-knowing, the five psychological energy centers vibrate at higher frequencies. Review the Energy Centers – Planets section in Chapter 2 on page **30**. The five psychological centers are the genital center (Jupiter), the solar plexus center (Mars), the heart center (Venus), the throat center (Mercury) and the third eye center (Moon).

There are nine diamonds. The first four energy centers have a positive and a negative polarity indicated by a larger masculine yang diamond complemented by a smaller feminine yin diamond. The ninth top diamond is paired with a triad image that includes a waxing crescent moon, a new moon and a waning crescent moon. Symbolically, the new moon stands for the mysterious, the subtle energies of intuition that reflect and resonate with the super-subtle conscious presence.

Three is a masculine, positive yang number. The largest four-sided diamond just below the moon triad represents the throat center. Four is a feminine

yin number according to Pythagorean numerology. When one
develops awareness of the psychological energies of instinct, desire
and feeling, the heart center
awakens to unconditional love
and the throat center (speech)
aligns with focused awareness in
the third eye.

The waning and waxing
crescent moons touch either side
of the new moon. The symbolism here signifies that the light
of awareness has penetrated
into the psyche. Note that of the
twelve images in the tattoo the
new moon is the only one that
is not totally black. There's an
emerging light seen in the central
part of the orb.

As one masters the five
psychological energy centers,
the spiritual frequencies, light
frequencies begin to slowly
permeate the psyche. As the
American master Vitvan writes,
"the description of the opening
and developing of these centers
constitutes the esoteric and basic
teachings of all advanced mystery
schools and does so down to this
day."

The diamond shape
represents the commitment to a
spiritual path leading to the even-
tual alchemical marriage of spiritual light with the dynamically

balanced psyche. Furthermore,
the manifestation of diamond
consciousness shows a capacity to
see multiple perspectives. Diamonds are multifaceted. Vitvan
writes of light regions, "Above
the Second Crossing [becoming
individuated] there are several
differentiated regions of light:
diffused light, diamond light
and supernal light. The diamond
light is pure, unreflected light."

The nine diamonds along
the spine figure prominently.
The Neo-Platonist, Thomas Tay-
lor, translated the Eleusian and
Bacchus mysteries from ancient
Greek into English. Regarding
the number nine he wrote,
Greek metaphysical science
asserts that the soul came down
through nine stages "and became
connected with the sublunary
world and a terrene body, as the
ninth and most abject gradation
of her descent." The lunar diamond tattoo reflects this ancient
Greek mythological theme.

From a descending view-
point the nine diamonds go from
larger to smaller. The power and
energies of the soul or psyche
decrease in potencies. The diamond at the top, as previously
mentioned, represents the conscious speech (throat center/Mer-
cury). The two diamonds at the

base of the spine symbolize the energy center that resonates with the reproductive drive.

The archetypal nine can also be found in the nine Greek mythological muses, the reference to the nine-gated city – two eyes, two nostrils, two ears, one mouth, the anus and genitals. Additionally, the early Gnostic Christian mystery schools used the Greek word Episteme meaning the highest degree of knowledge. Its numerical value is 999. Adding up the three nines equals 27. Two plus seven equals 9.

The fact that the lunar diamond tattoo runs along the spine must be addressed. On a physiological level the spine is the source of strength and energy. There are three major energy channels connected to the spinal column. On one side is the positive yang channel and on the other side the negative yin channel. The central channel is the neutral channel of empty space.

When one practices non-identification, there's greater balance. Nothing sticks to you. There's an opening to the free flow of life force. This in turn increases the rate of energy vibration in the centers ultimately allowing the spiritual energies to rise up from the tip of the tail-

bone to the apex of the thousand petaled lotus at the crown of the head.

Finally, the black color symbolism needs to be interpreted. Black, in fact, is not a color. Rather, it's the absence of color. Here black is associated with self-control, self-discipline, individuation and flexible will. As one masters their psychological energies, the psyche reflects the diamond light revealing life's mysteries and a deeper knowledge, understanding and wisdom.

Georgia Maestro – Lunar Diamond Tattoo

When Georgia was about 21 she had a lucid dream or what Carl Jung the Swiss psychologist called a 'big dream'. Georgia called it a vivid dream. In the dream, she viewed herself from behind. She saw the lunar diamond tattoo on her back as clear as day. Over the next few days, she made several sketches of the tattoo. She provided the tattoo artist her sketches. She recalls the dream occurred around her 21st birthday (2002). She recently had the tattoo touched up (2017).

Dr. Greg Nielsen, "Dr. G", & Dane Nielsen
From the Dane and DaddyPants National Parks & Golf Tour

Spiritual Frequencies Online Academy. Where you can become a patron for a modest monthly subscription. Go to Patreon.com/spiritualfrequencies for Dr. G's digital books, audio, video courses and more. New weekly uploads.

Patreon: patreon.com/spiritualfrequencies
Email: spiritualfrequenciesonline@gmail.com
Website: http://spiritualfrequencies.weebly.com/
Instagram: drgfrequencies
YouTube Channel: https://www.youtube.com/channel/UCA8Rw-m6Xl4C8D131dqAkeIw
Facebook: https://www.facebook.com/drgfrequencies
Venmo: contribute directly to Conscious Books & Spiritual Frequencies Online Academy Credit Union Account: @Greg-Nielsen-9

Conscious Books
316 California Avenue, Ste. 210
Reno, Nevada 89509
U.S.A.

The Awakening Series & book layout/design artist Cyndee Bogard: Cyndee's high school art teacher recognized and encouraged her creativity. After high school she attended college in Long Beach where she studied clothing design and merchandising. Later she enrolled at the University of Nevada-Reno studying Fine Art and Art History. There her talents found expression in metal sculpture, mixed media, and oil painting. Soon she began showing her work in the Reno/Tahoe and San Francisco Bay area. Shortly there after she wrapped up her formal education which includes an Advanced Certification in web design & marketing (Sessions Online Design School) while attaning her BS in Liberal Arts with a dual focus in Business Management and Visual & Performing Art (Excelsior University). You can learn more about Cyndee on her website: https://www.cyndeebogard.com or contact her via email: bcreativedesigns@gmail.com

If you would like a mythological interpretation of a tattoo or if you are interested in ordering Cyndee's *Awakening Series* prints please contact Dr. Greg Nielsen via email: spiritualfrequenciesonline@gmail.com

www.ingramcontent.com/pod-product-compliance
Lightning Source LLC
Chambersburg PA
CBHW072252270326
41930CB00010B/2353